Mind, Body, Spirit Workbook

DR CHRISTINE PAGE
MBBS, MRCGP, DCH, DRCOG, MFHom

and

KEITH HAGENBACH MA

Mind, Body, Spirit Workbook

A HANDBOOK OF HEALTH

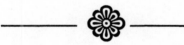

INDEX COMPILED BY ANN GRIFFITHS

SAFFRON WALDEN
THE C.W. DANIEL COMPANY LIMITED

First published in Great Britain in 1999
by The C.W. Daniel Company Limited
1 Church Path, Saffron Walden,
Essex, CB10 1JP, United Kingdom
2

ISBN 9780852073339

The Random House Group Limited supports The Forest Stewardship
Council (FSC), the leading international forest certification organisation.
All our titles that are printed on Greenpeace approved FSC certified paper
carry the FSC logo. Our paper procurement policy can be found at:
www.rbooks.co.uk/environment

Produced in association with Book Production Consultants plc
25-27 High Street, Chesterton, Cambridge, CB4 1ND, UK
Typeset by Cambridge Photosetting Services, Cambridge
Printed and bound in Great Britain by
Antony Rowe Ltd, Chippenham, Wiltshire

Contents

Introduction

Looking back, my decision to join the St John's Ambulance Brigade at the age of eleven, reflected an early desire to alleviate pain and suffering. On another level, it introduced me to a field of study which would become a life-time quest: the ability to harmonise and express all aspects of our being – mind, body and spirit.

The fact that I was always grateful that nobody became seriously ill during my shift of duty, also portrayed my sensitivity to the sight of blood and a tendency to slide gracefully to the floor in a dead faint on such occasions!

But despite this minor handicap, I entered the portals of the Royal Free Medical School, London, over 25 years ago, eager to pursue my chosen career. The fainting ceased as I learned to focus my thoughts on the needs of the individual and less on their suffering. Soon I was entranced by the complexity of the human being and its ability to adapt (or not) to any conditions in a unique and individual manner, which often defied logic.

Despite the long hours and inadequate consideration of the carer's needs, I thoroughly enjoyed my work especially when I found myself sharing the intimacy of a pivotal point in the life of another person. At this moment, we appeared to enter a place where time stood still, and yet, there was eternity; where decisions were required to be made, but there were abundant possibilities. In this magical place, in the gap between time and space, I witnessed true transformation on a soul level.

My natural curiosity and the desire to pursue the enquiries of a true scientist, led me from orthodox medicine into the field of the complementary therapies and especially homoeopathy. Within this structure, I was able to give more time to my patients and thereby gain a greater understanding of their state of dis-ease as they attempted to integrate their inner and outer lives.

I soon realised that restoring physical health without consideration of the mind and spirit, was merely placing a Band-aid over the problem, with disharmony emerging often at a later date in the same or different manner. And yet, the individual was often so unaware of the link between mind and body and their ability to influence the former, that education became a large part of my work.

About the same time, it became apparent that there was a strong correlation between personality types and specific illnesses and that disease seemed to appear when particular aspects of that personality were no longer in harmony with the deeper note of the soul. Illness therefore was not a weakness or failure but rather an attempt, by the individual, to restore a state of balance and growth. Illness, in short, is a *wake-up call*!

This concept was not always appreciated, as it was far more comfortable to imagine that some outside influence, such as a virus, had caused the illness, rather than to admit any intimate connection between oneself and the disharmony. This belief strongly paralleled that of the Middle Ages, when disease was believed to be caused by 'bad spirits'. I have even been accused of making patients 'feel guilty' by establishing such a link and that it was 'far kinder' to tell them that the illness had nothing to do with them, even though it was occurring in their body.

However, in my mind this approach discredited the inner intelligence of the individual and increased the sense of helplessness which was already present, especially in diseases of the immune system. Knowing we have choice and control over our lives asks that we accept personal responsibility but also empowers us as we learn to listen to, and follow, our own inner guidance or intuition.

In this way, we will then recognise when to ask for help, the type of help with which we resonate and how to work in cooperation with the doctor or therapist involved. Such an approach also requires each practitioner to look at the motivation behind their actions and ask whether it is one of facilitation or control. This is important at this time for, in my experience, there is no health service around the world which can survive the financial and personal demands of its clients, created, to a large degree, by a practitioner-dependent system and a focus on quantity not quality.

Throughout the years of my involvement with medicine, I have witnessed tremendous changes in health care. AIDS was unknown in the seventies and everything we knew about the immune system could be fitted into a slim publication; now there are thousands of papers and books on the subject. The art of surgery has been greatly refined leading to shorter lengths of stay in hospital following any operation and a move towards greater community involvement. And now, genetic engineering is beginning to take its hold on the future of medicine, evoking many ethical and moral issues.

All types of therapy have their place, but I believe it is time that the patient became a partner in respect to their health care aspiring to an expanded sense of well-being. In order for this to happen, we need to reawaken the Inner Healer who has slumbered happily, but not healthily, in the mistaken belief that health was a matter for the professionals.

This workbook enables the individual to re-establish a link with their own Inner Healer and to begin to understand how the mind, body and spirit can work together in order to create and maintain total health. The program asks you to donate time and space for this process of transformation and gives you permission to relinquish those beliefs and attitudes which no longer serve you and replace them with ones which satisfy a deeper soul need.

Even though some of the text is meant to challenge old concepts, I ask that there is no struggle but that you remember that life (and this process) can be an enjoyable experience!

Christine Page
Berkshire, U.K.
1999.

The Workbook Concept

One of the principal lessons I have learned from my experience in psychotherapy is that the insights, understandings and realisations which have the greatest power to transform people's lives are those *they reach for themselves*. In other words, reading or hearing about someone else's ideas, experience or wisdom, illuminating and helpful though it may be, is at best only a small part of the process of discovering our *own unique truth*.

Your workbook was conceived, designed and structured as a tool for those drawn to discovering their own path, and getting in touch with that *inner truth*. It has a great deal to offer to a wide range of people, but will have special value for you if you are committed to '*doing it for yourself*' rather than looking for someone else to '*do it for you*'.

Bear in mind the following points; they will help you gain the most enjoyment, satisfaction and fun from this book:

The more you put in ...

In this context, 'more' relates to openness, commitment and awareness rather than time, effort and determination.

- *Openness* signifies readiness to let go of old thought patterns and beliefs and interact with the exercises and processes contained here, in a spirit of exploration and discovery.

- *Commitment* is to your health, well-being and personal growth; the recognition that these are important and merit having energy devoted to them.

- *Awareness* is knowing not merely *what* you are doing, but *why* you chose that option from all those available.

... the more you will get out

Your rewards will be in the form of closer contact with and more profound understanding of your inner truth, wisdom and guidance. This process will manifest in your life in terms of increased energy levels, improved physical well-being and an enhanced capacity to respond to your inner guidance system rather than needing to look outside yourself to find out how to live life.

Suspend judgement ...

Holding on grimly to old belief systems is guaranteed to block the possibility of discovering new, stimulating and enriching perspectives on life.

- Put aside notions of 'right' and 'wrong'.

- Approach the work instead in a spirit of honouring and respecting 'whatever is'.

... work with your intuition

You have already started the process of listening to and working with your intuition by choosing this book. Here are some examples of how you can continue:

- We strongly recommend you create a journal in which to record the results of your experiential work. Rather than buying the first notebook you see, examine a variety of possibilities *and allow your intuition to guide your choice of the one which is right for you.*

- Repeat the process in choosing your pens, pencils, crayons or felt-tips.

- The selection of a special place in your home or garden in which to enjoy visualisations and meditations is an important one. *Why not experiment, trying out some alternatives and allowing yourself to respond to your inner sense of which one will best suit the purpose?*

Working with your Workbook

Information

Those parts of the text whose function is to inform or explain appear in typeface like this.

Questions

> Text in a box like this, contains questions for you to consider and answer. In some cases, it will include spaces intended for those answers.
>
> Depending on your mood at the time, or the nature of the questions, you may be tempted not to answer some of them.

Nobody (and certainly not us!) has the right to say you 'should' answer them. In this work, there are no shoulds and shouldn'ts, rights or wrongs.

Whatever your decision in relation to any particular exercise, however, take your time 'in awareness'. In other words, take time to consider the questions and, most important of all, your relationship to them. Be clear why you have chosen to do this particular exercise, or not. Do the questions challenge you in some way? Do you have strong feelings about them? The decision-making process itself may well carry a significant message for you – perhaps one worth recording in your journal and discussing with someone else.

Meditations and visualisations

Sections like this with borders left and right are perhaps the heart of this book. They are processes offering you an opportunity to 'still the ceaseless babble of the mind' and move into a unique world of imagination, instinct and intuition. Here you may discover personal truths, establishing contact with your Inner Healer and other dimensions of yourself whose help and guidance may prove invaluable.

Don't worry if you are unfamiliar with this kind of work. Approach it with trust, ready to honour and enjoy the unknown; you will be surprised at the richness of the inner world you discover.

We offer some practical advice on approaching and preparing for experiential work. However obvious or banal it may sound, we urge you to bear it in mind, and consider incorporating it in whatever pre-work ritual you may develop for yourself.

❋ GIVE yourself PLENTY OF TIME for exercises.

> 15–20 MINUTES IS USUALLY ADEQUATE. WHERE WE FEEL MORE MIGHT BE REQUIRED, WE INDICATE IT.
>
> TREAT EACH EXERCISE AS A GIFT TO YOURSELF — AND BE GENEROUS!

❋ FIND a place and a position for the work in which you feel relaxed and at ease. (Not, of course, whilst driving or using machinery!)

> HAVE FUN WITH THE PROCESS OF CHOOSING; RELY ON YOUR INSTINCTS TO TELL YOU WHEN YOU HAVE FOUND IT. THE OBVIOUS PLACE MAY NOT BE THE ONE YOU FINALLY SELECT.
>
> EXPERIMENT WITH POSITIONS. DO YOU NOTICE ANY DIFFERENCE BETWEEN WORKING LYING DOWN OR SITTING UP?
>
> IF YOU SIT, CHOOSE A CHAIR WHICH GIVES YOU GOOD SUPPORT IN AN UPRIGHT POSITION (AND REMEMBER IT MAY BE FOR UP TO 30 MINUTES AT A TIME!).

❋ AVOID intrusions and interruptions.

> RESPECT THE SENSITIVITY OF INNER WORK BY MAKING SURE YOU WILL NOT SUFFER THE SHOCK OF INTERRUPTIONS. SWITCH OFF THE MOBILE, PUT YOUR ANSWERPHONE ON DUTY, AND DO YOU NEED A NOTICE ON THE DOOR?

❋ FINALLY, treat these exercises like pieces of clothing. Put them on, wear them and see how they suit you. When you are thoroughly familiar with them, see if they are comfortable in their present form, or whether you instinctively feel to modify them in any way. If you do, go ahead and experiment. MAKE THEM YOUR OWN.

Please note...

***This is the manner we have chosen to highlight sections of
text we feel are particularly important or significant. We
instinctively feel that they contain some special truth or
wisdom, and therefore decided to draw them to your attention.
If they do not carry the same weight for you,
pass them by. Honour your truth by focusing on whatever
you find in the book which is in harmony with it.***

And now it's up to YOU ... !

It is terribly easy to take this kind of work so seriously we forget it can
be fun, too. If you catch some part of yourself worrying exactly how
you *should* do a section of the experiential work, try instead *making
it your own* – relying on your intuitive response to decide what will
work best for you – what will be most rewarding.

Don't forget that the value of the exercises is enormously
increased if they are carried out *on a regular basis*. The experience
will be different depending on, amongst other things, your mood,
state of health, emotional state and progress on your personal
journey. You may find you have favourites, but do not neglect the
others – your resistance to them may well embrace a gift for you!

... perhaps with friends

Doing experiential work in groups can be highly rewarding. If you
have family, friends or colleagues who are 'on your wavelength' why
not invite them to share the experience of some of the meditations
or guided visualisations? Discussing your individual experiences can
often throw fascinating new light on them.

Keith Hagenbach
Sussex, U.K.
1999

Psycho-neuroimmunology

'Your mind is in every cell of your body.'
CANDACE PERT

Recent work in the field of neurobiology has given solid scientific grounding to many widely-held intuitive beliefs underpinning the holistic approach to health and healing. Examples of such beliefs include:

A person's emotional state has a direct influence on their level of health.

A prerequisite for healing is trust in the healing process.

Changes of life-style can alter the progression of many diseases – even life-threatening ones.

Illness represents a pattern of disharmony which cannot be isolated from the person in whom it occurs.

One of the primary reasons why such concepts have struggled to gain acceptance in our culture is that they happen to run counter to the belief-system underlying mainstream Western medicine. To discover why this should be, we have only to turn our attention to the seventeenth century, and the work of French philosopher René Descartes.

The Cartesian view of living organisms – including human beings – asserted they could be treated as machines. It held that a person's body could be treated in isolation from their mind, spirit or emotions. In due course this doctrine, which also rejected anything which could not be seen, touched or physically felt, became part of the basis of modern science and Western medicine.

The wide acceptance it gained is all the more extraordinary when we remember the model offered by Descartes ran directly counter to the prevailing beliefs of his time. It represented a movement away from faith and also conflicted with the teaching of the Church.

Fritjof Capra writes in his book *The Turning Point:*

'Before Descartes, most healers had addressed themselves to the interplay of body and soul, and had treated their patients within the context of the social and spiritual environment ... Descartes' philosophy changed this situation profoundly. His strict division between mind and body led physicians to concentrate on the body-machine, and neglect the psychological, social and environmental aspects of illness.'

The Cartesian perspective gained such enormous power and influence that over 300 years passed before it was seriously challenged. It is interesting to note that the challenge has come from 'alternative' or 'complementary' medicine which is itself based on knowledge and understandings predating the ideas of Descartes by many centuries.

One of the most striking examples of this shift in perception is provided by **psychoneuroimmunology** (or **PNI**). This fledgling branch of neurobiology has shown that any attempted separation of mind from body flies in the face of present scientific knowledge, for it has provided proof that *the body literally contains the mind.*

Neuropeptides

Until about 20 years ago, it was universally accepted within the medical profession that 'body-information' was transmitted **neurally** – passed from nerve to nerve. This picture was radically transformed by the work of medical scientists like neurobiologist Candace Pert, the principal pioneer of PNI. They theorised and subsequently proved the existence of chemicals called **neuropeptides** (also known as *neurotransmitters* or *informational molecules*).

Triggered by our emotions, they circulate in the fluid components of the body (such as tears, sweat and blood) acting as messengers between the mind and various parts of the body, including the immune system. As such, they are in essence *thoughts transformed into matter.* There are at present 60 known neuropeptides, each related to a different emotion, of which **happiness**, **fear**, **sadness** and **anger** are amongst the most potent.

The first neuropeptide identified was **endorphin**. A natural morphine, it is commonly triggered to act as a pain-killer when the body experiences very high levels of pain. In emergencies, when enormously increased levels of physical strength are required, endorphin is also capable of enabling an individual to perform 'super-human' feats. This is the explanation of reports of such accidents as when a child is trapped under a car, and a slender mother somehow finds the strength to lift the car long enough for the child to be released.

Depending on the nature of the neuropeptide, it may trigger:

a) a release of hormones
b) an increase or decrease in the size of a cell or group of cells
c) increased or decreased function of a cell or group of cells.

Neuropeptides are produced and used extremely rapidly, causing a specific change in cell activity. If the normal response of a particular cell to the release of the neurotransmitter triggered by a specific emotion is to grow, then when the emotion is 'released' or 'expressed', the cell should return to its normal size.

If, however, the emotion is 'held' (some experts suggest for as little as five days) rather than released, the increased level of cell growth may continue. An imbalance in body chemistry created in this way – if sufficiently radical – may eventually result in the development of a tumour. Although only one amongst a number of factors, it will be seen that the emotional component of disease causation is of great significance.

In other words, *we need to express the appropriate emotion at the appropriate time*. If we do so, all is well. Too often, however, that crucial process is neglected or only partly completed, leaving a time-bomb ticking away within our system.

It is a major step towards maintaining levels of health to bear in mind:

'Holding on' may be a principal cause of illness

while

The seeds of healing on all levels are found in learning to let go.

One of the most revolutionary – some would say heretical – aspects of PNI was the understanding that cells communicate with one another *without the involvement of the brain*. Neurotransmitters are released from *all* parts of the body, and the result is interconnectedness at a cellular level, quite independent of the brain function.

Previously it had been believed that cells' receptor sites for neuropeptides were located exclusively in the brain and nerve tissue. Now, thanks to the research findings of Candace Pert and her colleagues, these same sites have been found elsewhere, including in the bowel, the kidneys, the white blood cells, the endocrine system, and other aspects of the immune system.

It is quite clear neuropeptides are part of our body's 'information technology', and play key roles in the process (illustrated in the diagram below) by which our thoughts and feelings exert a direct effect on our physical systems.

Thoughts & emotions

lead to a release of neurotransmitters
from the brain and many other cells

these circulate in body fluids
until they reach their target organ or cell

the neurotransmitters fit into the receptor site on the cell
membrane (like a key into a lock)

their information is transmitted into the cell's nucleus, influencing
the cell's activity in a particular way which may be:

a) increase in production of hormones
b) increase/decrease in cell size
c) increase/decrease in cell activity.

PNI, seen as 'the science of mind–body connection' helps us understand how our life experiences are capable of affecting the state of well-being of our bodies. Charting the chemical changes in our system which result from changes in our feelings, we see incontrovertible proof of direct links between what we term the 'psychological' or 'emotional', and what we think of as 'physical'.

Taking this one step further offers a crucial understanding of the innate self-healing power of the body; it gives life and form to the concept of the Inner Healer (see Chapter on The Inner Healer).

If PNI helps to explain the process by which emotional and psychological imbalance manifest on the physical level, equally it demonstrates the degree to which healing on this same level can be facilitated by working on the imbalance or dis-ease at the emotional and psychological levels.

It recognises the role of faith, prayer and visual imagery in the healing process, and acknowledges that the seeds of healing are literally contained in the disease itself.

As Jungian analyst Albert Kreinheder expressed it: *'The paradox is that the wound is also the treasure.'*

There are a number of studies which demonstrate a strong immuno-logical response to emotion. These include the following examples:

- After viewing a film of the late Mother Teresa ministering to the poor in Calcutta, students showed increased levels of immunoglobulin A in their saliva. This indicates heightened immune system activity, strongly suggesting positive emotions can stimulate the immune function.

- In a study of medical students, levels of circulating lymphocytes (white blood cells) were diminished on the first day of final exams compared to control periods before and after the exams. This relates to fear of being out of control of the subject matter on the examination paper.

• Lymphocyte activity is diminished in males two months after the death of a spouse from breast cancer, compared with the general population who have not suffered such a loss of a loved one. It was interesting to note that immediately after the death, activity was normal. This suggests in the early stages of grieving the effect is not felt, due either to possible 'emotional numbness', or the fact we are often surrounded by support in the period immediately following bereavement.

(Schleifer S. *et al*. 'Suppression of lymphocyte stimulation after bereavement' *JAMA* 1983; 250[3])

The Inner Healer

*'For healing to occur, we must come to see that
we are not so much responsible for our illnesses
as responsible to them.'*

Dr Christiane Northrup

The **Inner Healer** is that part of us which knows wholeness, and seeks to re-establish this state whenever possible. From a spiritual perspective, inner healing can be described as the process by which we strive to reconnect and rediscover our sense of Unity.

It is important to remember our Inner Healer is much more than a force with the power to 'make us better' or 'cure' us in terms of taking away the symptoms of physical illness. Embracing the true concept of the Inner Healer means acknowledging its work at every level – spiritual, emotional and intellectual as well as physical.

Looking at the modern medical response to illness, we find the emphasis has invariably been on 're-covery', with all efforts focused on attempts 'to cover up again'. The Inner Healer asks us to adopt a very different approach, powerfully expressed by medical scientist Jean Achterberg:

'Call out your disease, set it in front of you. Acknowledge it, give it a story, a metaphor, a sound, a smell, a covering. Then get a picture of the internal process that can heal you.'

Rather than place a sticking plaster over the wound, we are prompted to honour and respect it; examine it, perhaps even give it a voice and encourage it to dialogue with us. (See p. 82 Voice dialogue with the body in the Chapter on The Opportunity of Illness.)

If we participate actively in this process, and are truly committed to it, we give ourselves an opportunity to experience fully what is going on at the material level. For many people, connecting fully with life on the physical level – although vital if we are really to 'be here' on the planet – is very challenging. For some, pain and sickness may be the necessary route to establishing that connection. Paradoxically, therefore, suffering may sometimes be a sign of the Inner Healer at work.

The exercise which follows is designed to help you make contact with and begin to get to know your personal Inner Healer. It will greatly assist the process to bear in mind that this is a part of you and, as such, is 'within' or 'internal' rather than being part of a 'higher' or separate expression of yourself.

You do not have to be ill or even feel in need of healing to benefit from this exercise! This expression of yourself is constantly available and accessible to you, irrespective of how you feel or your state of health.

Getting in touch with your Inner Healer

For this, as for any visualisation exercise, have a notebook and coloured pens or pencils handy so you can make a record of your experience. You may find it interesting and enlightening to refer to this record in the future.

Allow yourself plenty of time. You are entering the realm of imagination and dreams, which is not subject to time and space. (This makes it quite different from our normal waking state, which shamans call 'ordinary reality'.) To gain maximum benefit, find a space where you are comfortable, relaxed, and safe from interruption.

❊ WITH eyes closed, take a few deep breaths. As you exhale, have a sense of releasing any stress or tension in your system, letting it go with your breath. Repeat the process until you feel relaxed and ready to begin.

❊ BRING into awareness that energy within you which guides you lovingly along your soul path – the path leading to wholeness on all levels – spiritual, intellectual, emotional and physical. This energy is your Inner Healer.

❊ WHEN you have a sense of that energy, allow an image to emerge which represents it. It may be a man, woman, a religious figure you associate with healing, a bird, animal, or anything else in the Universe.

IF YOU FEEL THE NEED TO CREATE OR MANUFACTURE AN IMAGE, FOLLOW YOUR INSTINCT AND DO SO. TRUST THAT THERE ARE NO RIGHTS AND WRONGS – ONLY YOUR UNIQUE PERSONAL PROCESS.

❊ ONCE the image has formed, take time to get to know it; it plays an important role in your life. Be aware of its size, appearance and its colours. What are your feelings as you meet this image for the first time? Don't be disturbed if it changes its appearance in any way; it may need to show you different aspects of itself.

WITHOUT PROMPTING OR JUDGEMENT, GIVE THE IMAGE TIME AND SPACE TO REVEAL ANYTHING IT MAY WISH TO REVEAL ABOUT ITSELF. O YOU HAVE ANY SENSE OF A FEELING OR AN ENERGY EMANATING FROM IT?

❁   WHEN you feel ready to do so, talk to your Inner Healer. On this occasion it may have taken the form of an inanimate object, but in the realm you now occupy, even rocks and waterfalls have a voice!

❁   THE part of yourself with which you have connected cares very deeply for you. You are free to ask it any question you wish, drawing upon its wisdom and insight. Choose your questions with awareness; their quality has a direct bearing on the quality of the answer you receive.

IF YOU ARE ILL, YOU MAY LIKE TO CONSIDER QUESTIONS SUCH AS: WHAT CAN I LEARN FROM THIS ILLNESS? WHAT NEEDS TO CHANGE BEFORE HARMONY CAN BE RESTORED?

TAKE AS MUCH TIME AS YOU NEED; IN THIS WAY YOU GIVE YOURSELF THE OPPORTUNITY OF GAINING THE GREATEST BENEFIT FROM THE PROCESS.

❁   WHEN you feel complete, you may wish to ask your Inner Healer if there is any further message it wants to give you. This done, it remains only to thank this loving energy for its guidance in whatever way feels right to you.

❁   ONCE you are ready, return to 'ordinary reality' and open your eyes once more.

TAKE TIME TO MAKE YOUR RECORD OF THE PROCESS. DOING SO NOT ONLY ENHANCES THE TRANSFORMATIONAL POWER OF IMAGERY WORK, BUT ALSO PROVIDES A REFERENCE POINT WHICH ENABLES YOU TO TRACE THE DEVELOPMENT OF YOUR WORK ON THIS LEVEL.

The challenge of inner healing

Reference to the Chapter on Psychoneuroimmunology will provide further insight into how this branch of medical science validates the concept of the Inner Healer. The fact remains, however, that for some people, acknowledging and awakening this part of themselves may be a challenging process.

As already mentioned, it asks us to re-evaluate the degree of reliance we place on 'external' sources of healing – whether our friendly and familiar GP, the awe-inspiring and sometimes daunting hi-tech of the intensive care wards of big hospitals or our complementary practitioner.

The enlightened approach to healing lies not in turning our backs on these 'external' sources, nor in *substituting* the Inner Healer for other forms of medicine, but to view our own health care in terms of a *partnership* between the two.

In the case of someone suffering from lower back pain, for example, the immediate and pressing need is to engage in the appropriate tests in order to identify the cause of the problem on a physical level. This may be met by physiotherapy, manipulation, or pain-killers prescribed by a GP.

For someone who chooses to work with their Inner Healer, however, this would be only the beginning of the process. Their next step might be to dialogue with the part of the body in pain, exploring what message it is carrying.

It is commonly seen, for example, that a lower back problem signals the experience of feeling unsupported by others or fear of moving on. There is often unrealistically high expectation of self and others and resistance to asking for help accompanied by the belief that: 'If you want a good job done, do it yourself!' This might lead to the need to work on issues such as releasing expectations of others, allowing oneself to be supported by others and 'going with the flow'.

The Inner Healer is engaged when the urgent physical need has been met, and facilitates the process of discovering the message the person's body is trying to communicate and enabling change where appropriate.

Such changes are part of returning to our natural state – in other words to *TOTAL HEALTH*, which is inherent in our being. Simply by realigning ourselves to our Inner Healer, we are able to regain health without necessarily being aware of the cause of our disease. This process, however, requires a faith whose source is not our 'brain–mind', but emerges from a more profound level of knowing.

Taking responsibility for our health ...

Working with our Inner Healer requires us to take responsibility for our health and well-being. For those who equate 'taking responsibility' with 'taking the blame', this may represent a real challenge. To acknowledge we have an innate healing capacity is, for some people, tantamount to saying they are in some way '*to blame*' for their illnesses.

The source of the confusion may be failure to distinguish between conscious and unconscious processes. We do not 'create' sickness in the sense of making a conscious, rational choice. On the other hand, embracing illness as an opportunity for learning and personal growth requires a jump in consciousness.

It also entails letting go of the limitations we have imposed on ourselves about what we can achieve by giving full expression to our personal power – including the power to heal ourselves and possibly others, too.

... *and for the rest of our life*

Once we start to respond to the messages from our body, we invariably find we become more sensitive to intuitive messages about other areas of our life. These are often accompanied by such a sense of certainty that they cannot be denied.

Exciting and life-enhancing though this may be, it can also be scary if our upbringing and life experience have left us with a legacy of powerful messages tending to negate that inner strength or wisdom deeply connected to our unique soul's journey. Messages of this nature include:

* *You can't do it on your own.*
* *Think of others before thinking about yourself.*
* *Daddy (or Mummy, or Doctor) knows best.*
* *Leave it to the experts (and you're not one of them!)*

❀ In the course of your lifetime experience, you may have picked up messages similar to these, negating your innate strength or wisdom. Jot some of them down in the spaces provided below:

....

....

....

....

....

....

Facilitating the process of inner healing

Awakening the Inner Healer is about trusting ourselves. In the exercise earlier in this Chapter, you were encouraged to make contact and dialogue with your Inner Healer. Your responses to the following questions will help you to identify potential barriers to activating that part of you.

Be honest. Sit with the questions. Allow the answers to emerge from the depth of your awareness rather than your brain or intellect.

> ✺   Do you believe you have the right to enjoy full health?
>
> ....

Any doubts or reservations you may have on this score will certainly show up in the level of your health. Accepting full health as your birthright is essential to achieving it.

> ✺   Are you comfortable with the concept of illness carrying
>   important messages from our soul?
>
> ....

One of the activities of the Inner Healer is to bring to our awareness messages from the soul which may be expressed in physical terms by the body. To work effectively with them means accepting these messages – and therefore the illnesses – as gifts. Ultimately, the purpose of the Inner Healer is to heal.

Many of those in the healing and caring professions find it challenging to acknowledge the importance of their own needs. Yet it is undeniably

❀   Is it easier to look after other people before attending to your own needs?

....

true that they can do most for others when they are healthy, happy and fulfilled in their own lives.

❀   Do you accept your mind, body and spirit as inseparable in terms of the healing process?

....

The separation of mind, body and spirit which became accepted following Descartes and Newton, was largely responsible for the decline of our trust in inner healing. The Inner Healer sees the broader picture and does not get caught up in the purely physical or material.

❀   Are you excited by the fact that at any time you can take full responsibility for decisions regarding your health and well-being with the help and guidance of health care experts?

....

Awakening and activating the Inner Healer asks us to step into our own power and begin a healthy partnership with the experts.

❀   Are you ready and willing to listen to and respond promptly to body messages knowing that the power and encouragement of the Inner Healer fully supports you?

....

'Listening to' or 'tuning in to' the body is an essential first step in working with and through the Inner Healer. In this way we learn to recognise disharmony promptly, rather than requiring it to manifest in the body in order to gain our attention.

Enjoy working with this magical friend ... !

Stress

*'Stress induced illnesses have now replaced infectious
diseases as the most prevalent health afflictions
affecting the industrialised nations.'*

LEON CHAITOW – YOUR COMPLETE STRESS-PROOFING PROGRAMME

In this Chapter, we will look at various aspects of stress, including:

- What is it?
- What causes it?
- How do we know if we are suffering from it?
- What can we do about it if we are?

The main text offers theories and understandings, but you will
also come across a wide variety of exercises. These provide the all-
important **experiential** element. By choosing to complete them you
will create an opportunity to:

- Determine your own relationship to stress
- Identify your own response to it
- Determine practical ways of dealing with it.

The conventional approach ...

STRESS became a buzz-word in the 1970s; all kinds of ailments and illnesses from insomnia to heart attacks were ascribed to it. Having virtually turned it into a disease in its own right, the next step was then to look for ways to treat it. Too often, however, what was accomplished was no more than suppression of the physical manifestations, often with the aid of prescribed drugs. These, effective though they may be in 'curing' the *symptoms*, do little to address the underlying causes of the problem.

... and from a different perspective

Focusing as it does on symptoms, the conventional approach overlooks important information on which the modern, more enlightened approach to stress is based:

A certain level of stress is natural, beneficial and even essential to life. Stress does not have to be bad – it may actually tell us we are alive!

Following a serious heart attack, a previously extremely healthy and lively octogenarian carefully avoided stressful situations – and found he became increasingly bored. Finally, risking a mild level of stress, he was amazed (and delighted) to discover that the adrenalin started flowing again. 'I felt a million dollars!' he reported.

Recent research has shown that our mechanisms for coping with stress are highly efficient and that even techniques such as relaxation and meditation may actually impair an individual's ability to use stress creatively.

Stress becomes a problem only when it produces a situation in which someone is 'stretched beyond their natural limits'. At this point STRESS becomes STRAIN.

This occurs when either:
there is a perceived threat to the person's physical or psychological well-being
or
the individual believes they are unable to cope with the situation.

Since it is our beliefs and perceptions which govern our response to stress it follows that:

The level at which the effects of stress become negative differ from person to person. Depending on their previous life experiences, some people possess a greater capacity than others to cope with stress.

Common 'stress-triggers'

See if you feel whether any of these mechanisms are relevant to your own experience. You may recognise elements of more than one, but if so, don't despair – the same is true for practically everyone!

1 The desire to be perfect

This one crops up in all kinds of guises. Even if you don't say it yourself, you must have heard people say 'Oh, I'm a perfectionist ...'.

It is usually said with pride, but it may be valuable to pause for a moment to think what it really means.

Because the sense of 'failing' is so strong, they can also be seen as 'thin-skinned' or acutely sensitive to anything they perceive as criticism. Fearful of not being 'good enough' they often seek to counter their feelings of insecurity by striving to be seen as strong, capable, and in control.

❀   What does perfection mean to you?

		Yes	No
1	Do you ever describe yourself as a perfectionist?	....	....
2	Do you judge yourself by other people's opinions of you?	....	....
3	Is it uncomfortable to let people see you just the way you are, 'warts and all' – or do you wear a mask?	....	....
4	Do you find it hard to admit you are wrong or that you have made a mistake?	....	....
5	Do you *have* to wash up that last cup before going out or going to bed?	....	....
6	Do you avoid starting things for fear of not doing them 'perfectly'?	....	....
7	Do you have high expectations of yourself (or others) which are often disappointed?	....	....
8	Do you fear 'not being good enough'?	....	....

If you have answered 'yes' to any of these questions it probably means THE DESIRE TO BE PERFECT is a primary cause of stress for you.

It also means that, somewhere along the line, you may have taken on board some pretty unrealistic pictures of how you need to be within the world, such as:

- It's not OK to make mistakes. (Tough, if you happen to be a human being!)

- It's not OK to let people see you the way you really are. You must invest a great deal of energy in creating and maintaining the false image of 'perfection'.

- You believe you can fool people into seeing you as something which, in truth, you are not. (There's often a subtle arrogance in this one!)

- Perfection lives in the future. 'I'll be fine when ...'

Although many of us spend enormous quantities of energy on it, the struggle for perfection based on a perception of how others see us is deeply unrewarding.

Why go on pursuing a mythical state we have created in response to familial or social norms?

REMEMBER ...

Life can be transformed as we learn to accept ourselves as perfect just the way we are.

---

2 The desire for approval or acknowledgement

This is the kind of approval you seek from the *outside* – from *other people*. But when you do not approve of or like yourself, it is hard to receive or believe the praise or approval offered by other people. The core problems here are:

- Do you *really* believe you are OK?
- Do you have genuinely *strong self-esteem*?
- Can you accept yourself *unconditionally*?

❋ **Do you crave approval or acknowledgement?**

		Yes	No
1	Do you ever find yourself asking for approval or acknowledgement with questions like: 'Did I do a good job?' 'Do you really think I look OK?' (And then find yourself disappointed by the reply?)	....	....
2	Is 'duty' important to you – do you sometimes do things you don't really want to do because you feel it's your duty?	....	....
3	Does it annoy you when you feel other people are being manipulative?	....	....
4	Do you ever demand love from others which you then don't receive and as a result feel hurt and let down?	....	....
5	Do you ever become inwardly resentful when you do something for someone else but fail to receive the acknowledgement or reward you think you deserve?	....	....
6	Do you have a 'need to be needed' or a 'need to be liked'?	....	....
7	Do you find yourself saying or doing what other people want and then feeling inwardly resentful?	....	....
8	Do you ever feel 'everything is my fault' and then spend time feeling guilty?	....	....

Answering 'yes' to any of these questions indicates your actions may sometimes be triggered by a deep-seated DESIRE FOR APPROVAL.

There is nothing strange or odd about this mechanism; most of us display signs of needing approval in some form from time to time.

This mode of acting almost certainly relates to childhood, when we tried to find ways to please the important people in our lives, those on whom we depended for our very survival. A poor sense of self may have developed when there was constant disapproval, lack of encouragement, or warmth. Now, however, we are adults; we can choose our own path.

REMEMBER ...

We do not have to waste our precious energy seeking external approval, which often prompts us to act in ways which do not serve us. We can choose instead to develop the ability to value and approve of ourselves.

Rather than giving our power away and becoming victim to others by blaming them for whatever is missing from our lives, we can enjoy creating it ourselves!

---

3 The desire to be in control

Many people feel safe only through believing they are *in control* – of themselves, of other people, of their environment and perhaps all three. There are many ways of seeking to establish control in this context, some of them obvious, others more subtle and less easy to recognise.

I wonder what you would fear changing or losing that would make you feel out of control? For example: work, money, your mind, family, friends, independence, structure.

❀ Take at least two minutes to stop and connect not only with
the thought of losing something or going out of control, but
with the feelings which surface. Record them, in as much
detail as you can, in the space below:

....

....

....

....

....

....

❀ **Do you seek excessive control in your life?**

		Yes	No
1	Do you avoid confrontation because you feel people might become aggressive if you upset them?	....	....
2	Do you have a tendency to tell others how to behave, and register your disapproval strongly if they decline your suggestions?	....	....
3	Have you organised your life (people and things) in the hope you will know exactly how things will turn out? (And then panic when the unexpected crops up?)	....	....
4	Do you find it difficult to be spontaneous?	....	....
5	Once you have taken a view or a position on something, do you become obstinate when challenged?	....	....
6	Do you ever feel your life would work better for you if it were not for the actions of others – such as your family, your partner, or the government? (Have you become a victim to the outside world?)	....	....
7	Do you fear change?	....	....
8	Do you need to make meticulous plans or endless lists?	....	....

These traits are characteristic of those who experience a powerful urge TO BE IN CONTROL.

Trying to establish control is an attempt to *eliminate the unexpected*. For those whose early life experience may have included an uncomfortable amount of the *unexpected* (perhaps in the form of parents who were inconsistent or unpredictable in their responses) this is perfectly understandable.

Frequent changes in home situations may also lead to a need to gain control unnaturally. Seeking safety through control, however, like any other childhood mechanism carried into adult life, can be extremely limiting.

REMEMBER ...

The desire to control is based on fear of the unknown. The best way to counter fear is to develop TRUST.

A hallmark of controllers is rigidity and tension.
If you recognise these traits in yourself, begin to develop and experiment with your spontaneity and sense of play. *It can work wonders!*

The desire for perfection, control and approval all lead to an inner sense of helplessness.

By now you have probably been able to identify some of the causes of stress in your life. Now we shall look at a few well-known factors which are acknowledged as enhancing our ability to cope with stress.

For each of the following questions, rate yourself on a scale of 1–10, circling the number you feel describes you most accurately. Numbers range from 10, a definite and unambiguous 'yes' down to 1, an equally clear and uncompromising 'no'.

	Yes									**No**
❁ Do you have a good level of self-esteem?	10	9	8	7	6	5	4	3	2	1

Do you acknowledge all your wonderful qualities as a human being and like yourself?

❁ Do you have – and use – a good support system where people care for who you are, not for what you do?	10	9	8	7	6	5	4	3	2	1

Can you readily call on the support of family, friends and loved ones?

❁ Are you someone with a fighting spirit?	10	9	8	7	6	5	4	3	2	1

Are you the type who doesn't readily accept defeat?

❁ Do you acknowledge and work with the challenge of stressful situations rather than try to deny their existence?	10	9	8	7	6	5	4	3	2	1

Do you recognise that denying problems may ease things in the short-term but is likely to create health problems over a longer period?

❁ Do you have the capacity to give and receive compliments freely and truthfully, or do you brush aside praise?	10	9	8	7	6	5	4	3	2	1

Are you able to acknowledge the special qualities which earn you those compliments?

Add up the value of the numbers you circled to find your total score.

Below 25: Improving your coping skills would enhance your quality of life.

Between 26–34: You have average coping ability.

35 or more: You seem to cope pretty well with stress.

These coping mechanisms are very successful, and their power to enhance health is proven. The next step is to recognise the signs of strain before they manifest in painful symptoms.

The better you know yourself, the better equipped you will be to deal with the underlying causes of stress. *THIS BOOK IS DESIGNED TO HELP YOU IN THAT PROCESS.*

The 'three Cs', coined by Suzanne Ouellette, provide another way of looking at coping abilities.

Answering the following questions will give you additional insight into the nature of your response to stress, and how well you are likely to be able to cope with its effects. Take a few moments when you have completed the exercise to get a sense of what your answers mean in terms of the level of stress you experience.

CHALLENGE

Do you view challenging experiences as:

a) danger?

b) opportunity?

c) something else? (If so, what?)

....

....

....

Escaping from some kind of threat do you feel you are running:
a) towards safety
b) away from danger?
c) something else? (If so, what?)

....
....
....

Does your view of the universe identify it as:
a) a friendly environment?
b) a dangerous or threatening one?
c) something else? (If so, what?)

....
....
....

❁ CONTROL

	Yes	No
Do you have a sense of personal power – the ability to handle whatever challenges life may offer?	....	....
Do you have a sense of purpose in your life experience?	....	....
Is the ultimate power in your universe:		
a) benevolent	....	....
b) arbitrary and unpredictable?	....	....
c) something else?	....	....

> ❀ **COMMITMENT**
>
> | | Yes | No |
> | --- | --- | --- |
> | Do you have vision and purpose? | .... | .... |
> | Is there clear intent behind everything you do? | .... | .... |
> | Is your life leading somewhere? | .... | .... |
> | | | |
> | Do you have a real desire to enjoy life to the fullest, and manifest your personal truth? | .... | .... |

Whatever your responses to these questions may be, DON'T BE DISAPPOINTED OR DISHEARTENED! Learning to deal with the pressure, stress and tension in our life is just like anything else – A MATTER OF FINDING THE METHODS WHICH WORK FOR US.

The 'memory' of stress

The exercise which follows demonstrates how quickly the body and mind adapt to thoughts — even those relating to past rather than present experiences. It is well suited to individual or group work. In the latter case, only the group leader or facilitator need be familiar with the process. If you are alone, however, simply study the steps for a few minutes until you feel ready to work with them.

Remember **whenever** doing experiential work:

- Give yourself adequate time. 10–15 minutes is ideal in this case.

- Find a place in which you feel relaxed and at ease. If you choose to sit, select a comfortable chair which provides good support to sit in a relaxed position, feet resting on the ground. (You may like to remove your shoes, and loosen any tight clothing.)

- Avoid interruptions or distractions; why not allow yourself to enjoy the full benefit of any inner work you undertake?

❀   CLOSE your eyes. Take a few deep breaths, breathing in through the nose and out through the mouth.

> DURING THE OUTBREATH, HAVE A SENSE OF LETTING GO OF ANY TENSION IN YOUR BODY.

❀   ALLOW your mind to drift back to the last time you experienced pressure or tension in your life. It doesn't have to be something major – but it might be. To the degree it is comfortable for you, allow the details of that situation to come back to you.

> SOME PEOPLE MAY FIND IT HELPFUL TO IMAGINE THAT THEY ARE WATCHING A VIDEO OR FILM OF THE EVENT, INCLUDING, OF COURSE, THEIR OWN INVOLVEMENT.

❀   AS you recall this stressful experience, become aware of how you feel. What is the nature of your emotional response? Does it make you feel angry, fearful, sad, or perhaps powerless?

❀   ALLOW yourself to be aware of any physical sensations related to the feelings you experience. Is there a lump in your throat, tightness in your chest, or maybe an ache around your heart?

✲ WHEN you feel ready, allow the stressful scene to evaporate, breathing out the feelings.

YOU SUMMONED THE MEMORY OF THOSE UNCOMFORTABLE FEELINGS IN ORDER TO LEARN FROM THEM, BUT YOU NEED NOT HOLD ONTO THEM ANY LONGER.

✲ ALLOW a new situation which is pleasant and stress-free, to replace the previous one. As you do so, be aware of how different this experience is from the previous one. Once more, breathe out the feelings.

WHEN YOU HAVE COMPLETED THE PROCESS, GENTLY OPEN YOUR EYES AND RETURN TO FULL AWARENESS.

It is highly recommended you make notes as a brief record of the process so you can refer to them later.

....
....
....
....
....
....
....

In the course of that exercise you will have been aware of certain *emotions*, along with associated *physical sensations* which may have changed, depending on whether you felt under strain or relaxed. Acknowledging and identifying these is an important step in determining your unique response to stress.

---

*Depending on your constitution or make-up, the nature of
these responses will have a significant influence on your
health, both physical and mental.*

The relationship between activity and varying levels of stress is
illustrated by the **Hans Selye Curve** shown below:

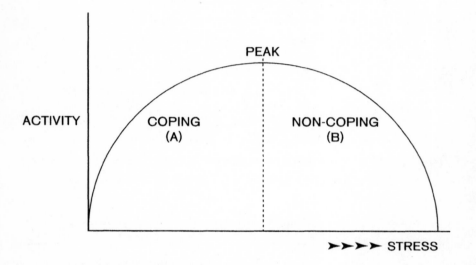

In section (A) the individual responds to increasing levels of stress *in
the short-term* in positive, or beneficial ways. In section (B) 'burn out'
sets in. In other words, hormonal responses to stress which were
positive in the short-term now begin to have a marked *negative* effect.

Adrenaline (the short-term stress hormone)

You may already be familiar with the **'fight or flight' response** with
which humans, in common with many animals, are equipped for their
protection. When we are faced with danger, this instinctive mechanism
prompts us either *to stand our ground and fight* or *save ourselves
by running away*.

Adrenaline's *positive* short-term physical effects include *increases* in:

- brain alertness
- heart rate and blood flow
- respiratory rate
- muscle tone
- visual acuity
- sweating

with corresponding *reductions* in:

- activity of intestines and stomach
- activity of the urinary system
- sexual hormones and urges
- temperature in fingers and toes.

In the longer term, however, the effects of the hormone can become *negative*.

	Short-term	Prolonged
Respiratory system	Increased oxygen supply	Hyperventilation, asthma
Nervous system	Increased level of alertness	Insomnia, mental overactivity
Heart	Increased heart rate and blood supply to vital organs	Palpitations, irregular heart beat, angina
Muscles	Primed for physical action	Aching, tension headaches
Eyes	Heightened visual acuity	Eye strain
Skin	Releases excess heat	Inappropriate sweating, body odour
Intestines	At times of stress, these parts of the	Peptic ulcers, indigestion, diarrhoea
Urinary system	body receive reduced blood supply so the	Kidney stones, frequent urination
Hands, feet	more essential organs	Cold hands and feet
Sex organs	can be supplied	Impotence, infertility

Cortisone

Beneficial short-term effects of **cortisone** include:

- increased blood sugar available as energy from the breakdown of stored fats, proteins and sugars
- decreased sensitivity to stressors
- increased ability to interpret and integrate
- increased physical energy.

A parallel from the natural world of Nature is provided by the hunting cat: focused on its prey, its body provides energy to the vital organs, enhancing its ability to interpret and integrate, while reducing awareness of other stressors or stimuli outside its field of vision.

Changes like these are vital for our survival in the *short-term*. Under continually stressful situations *long-term*, however, the effects are likely to become deleterious and sometimes even dangerous.

- *The increase in blood sugar levels can, if prolonged, lead to diabetes.*
- *There is a decrease in the immune response, heightening risks of infection and tumour formation.*
- *High levels of mental alertness can degenerate into insomnia and even psychosis.*

The challenge is to recognise when you reach the peak of the curve, between coping and non-coping.

It is extremely valuable to be able to recognise that moment and clues may be seen in the way you hold or move your body and in certain physiological or perhaps behavioural changes.

Take a few moments to identify your particular signals –
which may be physical, or psychological – and record them
in the space provided below:

Physical	Psychological
....	....
....	....
....	....
....	....
....	....
....	....
....	....

Common indicators include:

Physical: sweating, tension, nausea, feeling cold, tiredness

Psychological: irritability, crying, need to withdraw, frustration, loss
of energy

Our **behaviour** is subconsciously triggered by our **emotions** which
are, in turn, driven by our **beliefs.**

BELIEF

EMOTION

BEHAVIOUR
(physical)

If we can identify the signs of non-coping at the moment they arise,
we can choose to change our behaviour and the emotions which are
evoked and then start to understand the belief which underlies the
problem.

For example: you are working busily at your desk, with telephones ringing – but you are coping. Then someone walks in and 'dumps' a pile of letters in front of you, telling you they need to be answered immediately. Suddenly you feel sweaty, irritable and confused. You feel like walking out.

First aid measures

> Earlier in this Chapter, in 'The Memory of Stress' exercise, you reconnected with a stressful experience. Tune in to it again, briefly, and note which First Aid measures would have helped. What could you have changed?

1 Recognise the behaviour – and change it

Having identified the point at which you cease to cope, you are now in a position to modify your response, choosing to *do something different* so that you *maintain effective functioning* rather than 'going into overload'.

For each of us the answer will be different. The following examples illustrate common instinctive responses to stressful situations, and how they may be modified.

Holding your breath.
Quick or shallow breathing.

Move the energy down towards your feet as you breathe out. Just concentrating on your feet as you exhale will deepen the breath.

Crossing your arms across the solar plexus.	Move your hand down to your lap or side, turning the palms towards the other person. This signifies openness while straightening your back and renewing confidence.
Turning your gaze away from the other person.	Try to maintain eye contact. Allow your eyes to 'soften' by imagining something at which you would normally smile (children, a lovely view, or a playful animal).

For some the antidote may be to verbalise their feelings clearly and calmly.

For others the answer may lie in changing their posture by moving their arms, turning their hands, lifting their head or just smiling.

Others may find relief in standing up and walking around.

❀   Which 'First Aid' measures do you feel would have been of most help to you in countering stress in the situation you recalled?

....

....

....

....

2 *Recognise the emotion – and change it*

> ✿ What were you feeling? Recognise the emotion. Give it expression if necessary, and then let it go.
>
> ✿ Does your emotion need expression? If so, how could you do this, and then release it?
>
> ....
> ....
> ....
> ....

3 *Recognise the belief – and change it*

It is important to identify the beliefs which produce this kind of behaviour, and to remember this situation is often just one in a series of similar experiences which create a pattern. Keeping a journal is invaluable in helping you recognise such patterns. Record in your journal particular events or individuals who *repeatedly* create stress or strain in your life. Jot down what the triggers may be at such moments. Do you feel out of control, not good enough, criticised or discouraged?

> ✿ What beliefs underlie your stress?
>
> ....
> ....
> ....
> ....

Having recognised them, we can choose to change the beliefs using positive affirmations like those given below to reinforce the new ideas.

Perfection: 'I choose to love, value and care for myself exactly as I am, right now.'

Control: 'I trust the process of life. I choose to express myself fully and spontaneously, knowing I am safe.'

Approval: 'I acknowledge my unique qualities as a human being. I love and approve of myself.'

Learning to recognise the physical and emotional signs which tell us we have passed the point of peak performance and are moving into 'burn-out' will help us safeguard our health and well-being.

Progressive relaxation

Relaxation exercises have been found to be beneficial by countless people of all nationalities, cultures and beliefs throughout the planet. Overwhelming evidence suggests that such exercises, including many forms of meditation, possess powerful stress-relief properties. They are now used, not only in people's homes, but also in hospitals, hospices and even prisons. Try this one for yourself:

Once you are familiar with the simple steps shown below, you can enjoy this exercise on your own, or as a member of a group. You may wish to sit or lie down but if you have a tendency to fall asleep when lying down, it helps to bend your knees with your feet resting comfortably flat on the ground.

Twenty to thirty minutes is an ideal time to allow for this exercise. Don't forget that depriving ourselves of the time and space we need for relaxation is itself an underlying cause of stress. **And don't forget to avoid intrusions. Put a sign on your door if necessary, turn on the answerphone and switch those mobiles OFF!** Some people find playing soothing, relaxing music enhances their state of relaxation.

❁ CLOSING your eyes, signal to your system it is time to slow down by taking a few long, deep breaths – in through the nose, out through the mouth.

SOME PEOPLE FIND IT HELPFUL TO MAKE A SOUND AS THEY EXHALE. FOCUSING YOUR AWARENESS ON YOUR BREATHING WILL AID THE PROCESS.

❁ WHEN you feel ready to begin, allow your awareness to move down to your feet. Become aware of any tension in them. Relax and release it on the outbreath.

YOU MAY FIND IT AIDS THE PROCESS TO TIGHTEN EACH MUSCLE TO EXPERIENCE TENSION, WHICH IS THEN RELEASED.

❁ WORK your way slowly up the body, repeating the process for each group of muscles in turn – up to and including your scalp.

MAKE IT A GENUINE TIP-TO-TOE EXERCISE. WORK CONSCIOUSLY WITH CALVES, THIGHS, BUTTOCKS, STOMACH, SHOULDERS, ARMS ETC.

MAKE A MENTAL NOTE OF ANY PART OF THE BODY WHERE YOU FOUND IT DIFFICULT TO ACHIEVE RELAXATION, BUT DON'T DWELL ON IT OR WORRY ABOUT IT. IT'S NEITHER RIGHT NOR WRONG, GOOD NOR BAD — IT'S JUST THE WAY YOU ARE AT THIS PARTICULAR MOMENT.

❀ WHEN you reach a state of freedom from stress and tension, allow yourself to remain there and enjoy the experience.

ALLOW YOUR MIND TO FOLLOW THE BODY INTO A STATE OF PEACE AND CALM.

❀ BRING to mind an image of a 'safe place' in Nature and enjoy being in that place. It may be somewhere you know, or it may come from your imagination. Take time to become familiar with the surroundings, the appearance, textures, colours, sounds and scents.

❀ IN the safe place you can be yourself, free of expectations, concerns, guilt, or plans for the future. There is only <u>now</u> in this place, and Nature surrounds you, providing nourishment for your soul, mind and body.

REMAIN IN THIS STATE FOR AS LONG AS IS COMFORTABLE. DON'T HURRY. BE AWARE THAT SIMPLY BY 'SWITCHING OFF' AND LETTING YOUR BODY AND MIND RELAX, YOU ARE ALLOWING NURTURING AND HEALING TO TAKE PLACE.

❀ WHEN you feel ready to do so, allow yourself gently to return to 'everyday reality', but knowing the safe place is there for you always and ... open your eyes.

KEEP A NOTEBOOK HANDY TO JOT DOWN AREAS WHERE RELAXATION WAS DIFFICULT. SUCH RECORDS WILL HELP YOU SEE WHAT CHANGES OCCUR OVER TIME.

Please remember ...

Those of you unfamiliar with relaxation exercises may find the process slightly uncomfortable at first. For all its simplicity, if your normal mode of living is to keep constantly busy and live under tension, letting go in this way may not come easily. If this is the case, don't worry! It will come - with practice.

And you will find the rewards of that practice are enormous. Releasing yourself from the search for *perfection*, desperate efforts to win the *approval or acknowledgement* of others, or vain attempts to exert *control* releases a reservoir of energy you can use to enrich your experience and enhance your enjoyment of life. In other words, it is one of the greatest gifts you can give yourself. But don't take my word for it - try it!

The Opportunity of Illness

*'The key question in all diseases is
what is the Self trying to get me as a
patient to learn about myself?'*
BERNIE SIEGEL

For anyone raised in a society which devotes so much energy and so many resources to trying to 'make people better' when they become ill, the idea that illness may in fact represent a precious opportunity can come as something of a shock. A clue to the truth is supplied by the word 'health' which is derived from the Greek for 'wholeness'. This signifies complete functioning on all levels; not the physical alone, but also the mental, emotional and spiritual.

Much modern Western medicine is grounded in the Cartesian notion of the radical separation of body and spirit, and aims to do no more than 'cure' the physical symptoms. More and more people, however, are embracing the understanding that illness has a much greater and deeper significance than the exclusively physical.

Eastern medical wisdom offers a different perspective, illustrated by the words of Dr Chandra Sharma, once physician to Mahatma Ghandi: *'An illness is a self-representation of a human being at a stage at which something is demanded of him for the sake of experience.'*

In the past, smoking and viruses were seen as just two of the *causes* of disease. The new understanding, however, is that unresolved emotional issues, unexpressed emotions, limiting beliefs and even aspects of the soul's path do what Ken Wilber describes as 'prime the gun', while smoking and viruses do no more than 'pull the trigger', creating pathological changes.

❀ These ideas are wonderful as concepts, but when you or those close to you become ill do you ever fall back into seeing illness as weakness, failure, or even a deliberate attempt to gain attention?

and

❀ Can you embrace the possibility that illness is a wake-up call which contains in its own nature clues to its cure?

From the second perspective, the aim is no longer to eliminate signs and symptoms at all costs, but to study them for the clarity and direction they embody regarding the soul's path at that time. This view also accepts that illness may be offering the time, space and means by which we are able to leave behind a set of circumstances which are out of harmony with our soul, and return to our true soul path.

What is health – to you?

> Before reading this section, write down one sentence
> explaining what health means to you.
>
> ....
> ....
> ....

For many of us it is more than just physical well-being. We often
expect:

- peace of mind
- energy to achieve all we desire (and more)
- good relationships.

Can you be healthy when you are ill?

> If you have been ill for more than a few days, what did you
> ask for in terms of health?
>
> ....
> ....
> ....
> ....
> ....
> ....

❀   Was it more than:

   – just let me be able to sleep tonight ...
   – just let me be able to eat a little more ...
   – just let me be able to see the sun rise ...
   – let the pain not stop me doing the things I enjoy ...

❀   What would you need to be healthy when ill?

....
....
....
....
....

Our personal expectations of health depend on, amongst other things, our own experiences, and social, cultural and religious values – as well as our family values. In some families, for example, being ill is unacceptable.

It is significant that in our society the term often used for those experiencing illness is 'invalid'. By using this word do we also brand them 'in-valid' – of reduced value? Other prevailing social attitudes to disease and sickness are illustrated by terminology such as 'falling ill', 'suffering disease' or 'being a victim' to the condition.

What has been your experience of illness?

Family attitudes have a powerful influence on our relationship to illness.

❀ When you were a child, was it OK to be ill? ....
Were you given special foods? Was bed the place for
illness? (and was that exciting and special, or isolating?)

....
....
....
....

❀ Was there a need to produce physical signs of disease like
high temperature, spots or a broken limb before your
'illness' was considered genuine?..

....
....
....

❀ What was it like to have illness in your family (father, mother,
sibling or grandparents)?..

....
....

❀ When you were ill, did you receive extra attention and
sympathetic support (or did you feel 'punished' in some
way)?..

....
....

❀ Were your parents caring and supportive when you were ill,
or were you told (verbally or non-verbally) that illness was
inconvenient?..

....
....

❋ Was your father's response any different from your mother's?...
....
....

❋ When, as an adult, you are ill, do you see any similarity between your response and behaviour, and that of your parents?..
....
....

❋ Take time at this point to write down any further memories of how it was to be ill in your family.

....
....
....
....
....
....
....

❋ What effect did these experiences have on your life and your appreciation of and response to illness – your own or that of others?

....
....
....
....
....
....

Signs and symptoms

'Symptoms are potentially meaningful and purposeful conditions. They could be the beginning of fantastic phases of life, or they could bring one amazingly close to the centre of existence.'

ARNIE MINDELL

❋ **Write down your response to this quote from Arnie Mindell.**

....

....

....

....

....

From the holistic health perspective, illness is a vital part of the individual's *inner guidance* system; it has the potential to *show us the way forward.* To achieve a deeper understanding of this view requires that we examine an individual's needs on all levels – the physical, emotional, mental and spiritual.

Physical needs

> List what you consider to be a human being's seven most
> important physical needs.
>
> ....
>
> ....
>
> ....

How many of the following were included in your list?

- Food
- Fluids
- Warmth
- Fresh air
- Light
- Exercise
- Rest

The precise level of any individual's needs varies according to such things as expected availability and the physical environment. Whatever that optimum level may be, however, *long-term excess or deficiency in any one area is potentially damaging*.

Moderation in all things – with fun!

Emotional needs

The satisfaction of physical needs alone is not enough. Medical research is rich in studies of babies kept well-fed and warm, but denied cuddling, stroking and human connection. Invariably their rate of growth and development fails to match that of babies nourished both physically *and* emotionally.

For full emotional development to take place, individuals need the ability not simply to experience their emotions, but to *express* them. Research has repeatedly demonstrated the dramatic effect of appropriate expression on the person's biology.

In the book *Healing and the Mind*, Margaret Kemeny quotes the case of a group of actors chosen for their ability to express their own emotions with sincerity. After auditions, some were told they were to be given starring roles. They expressed delight, and blood tests showed their immune response to be enhanced. Others, told that their performances were so poor they should leave the theatre, became dejected and depressed.

When blood tests were taken from the latter group, it was expected that their immune response would be impaired. In fact, it was enhanced, just as the first group's had been.

Expression and release

Expressing our emotions can often feel risky; we may upset others, 'rock the boat', let others see us as we really are, or even run right out of control. Perhaps for you there are other constraints which prevent you from 'saying it like it is' where your emotions are concerned.

> ✺   List the factors which make it difficult for you to 'speak your truth' when your feelings about other people are involved.
>
> ....
>
> ....
>
> ....

Expression means being able to express the full range of emotions in ways which are:

*congruent with the situation,
expressed to the appropriate person (or people),
expressed at the appropriate time*

... and then released.

Releasing an emotion involves dealing with it at a level deeper than simply expressing it. This means processing it so thoroughly that we no longer have any energetic link either to the emotion or the situation which originally evoked it. If you hear yourself repeating the same story about an old hurt, or can still elicit feelings related to something which happened years before, it is a clear sign that however much the feelings may have been *expressed*, they have yet to be *released*.

For many people, *forgiveness* is a particularly challenging aspect of releasing. Forgiveness means letting go, but where pain and hurt inflicted by others are involved, it is sometimes hard to achieve. In this case it is important to remember that forgiveness does not mean condoning or excusing the actions of other people, but acknowledging you no longer wish to hold on to or be part of that experience. It is a process of *setting ourselves free,* and as such is important for soul growth.

This simple exercise will help you determine whether you have released the emotions relating to a particular experience:

> ✸ Think of a time you felt anger, sadness or fear. (Remember it complete with all the sounds and images which accompany it.)
>
> ✸ Can you still feel the feelings related to that event in your mind and body? Write down these feelings together with any associated body sensations or images.
>
> ✸ If the answer is yes, are you still holding onto the story, together with the emotions relating to it? Is it time to let go?

Most of us have a tendency - if indeed we relate consciously to our emotions at all - to concentrate on *experiencing* and *expressing* them. What we may not fully acknowledge is the crucial importance of our ability also to *release* them. The significance of this last part of the process becomes clear if we remember it has been suggested that:

Any emotion held longer than five days can result in physical and mental illness.

There is nothing wrong with experiencing *happiness*. On the contrary, it is an emotion for which most people strive, and which they usually enjoy in others. Nevertheless, like any other emotion, if not released it may well result in a mild form of *mania*.

FEAR held for too long leads to ANXIETY or WORRY.

✽ Listed below are symptoms related to these emotions. Tick those you feel are relevant to your own experience:

- The constant 'chatterbox' ....
- 'Floating anxiety' ....
- A never-ending list of 'what ifs' ....
- A strong alliance between caring and worrying ....
  ('It's because I care that I worry')
- A tendency to see everything as it relates to you ....
- Restlessness ....
- Waking with anxious thoughts ....
- Always preparing for 'the inevitable' ....
- Hair, nail and bone disorders ....
- Kidney and bladder (cystitis) problems ....
- Diseases of the ears (including tinnitis) ....
- Impatience, intolerance ....

SADNESS held for too long leads to DEPRESSION or DESPAIR.

✽ Listed below are symptoms related to these emotions. Tick those you feel are relevant to your own experience:

- Tiredness ....
- Lack of enthusiasm ....
- Lack of motivation ....
- Irritability ....
- Restlessness (hiding sadness) ....
- An addiction to busyness ....
- Aching muscles ....
- Disorders of lungs, sinuses, skin and large bowel ....

**ANGER *held for too long leads to* RESENTMENT *or*
BITTERNESS.**

 Listed below are symptoms related to these emotions. Tick
those you feel are relevant to your own experience:

Resentment
- 'I'm not complaining, but ...'   ....
- 'You would have thought ...'   ....
- 'I'm disappointed, let down ...'   ....
- Ligament disorders (sprains)   ....
- Eye, liver and gall-bladder problems   ....
- Tension in neck muscles   ....
- Tightness in tempero-mandibular joints – jaws and
  grinding teeth   ....
- Gout, fibroids, benign breast lumps   ....

Bitterness
- 'Bitter and twisted'   ....
- Unable to forgive   ....
- Desire for revenge
  ('I don't care ... but if I meet him I'll kill him')   ....
- Bitter taste in mouth   ....
- Chronic arthritis   ....

❈

Mental needs

Full access to our intellectual function is important to our health.
Logic, for example, is essential for focusing incoming spiritual

impulses and transmuting them into thought forms. Equally, it enables us to objectively define our emotional responses as belief systems. Applying the gift of logical thought in these ways serves us, but danger threatens when servant becomes master! Used inappropriately, logic can restrain and block both spiritual and emotional flow.

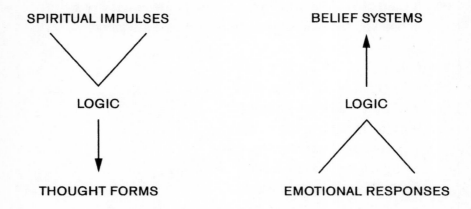

Ultimately, logic has an important role in our ability to make choices and take control of our life, although:

The *best choices* are made when we synthesize our feelings, logic and instincts, and use our intuition to bring wisdom and compassion to our decision making.

The *greatest control* results when we can release the need to control our physical world, our emotions, our thoughts and our beliefs, and trust in the security of inner knowing.

Finding the right balance between choice and control is essential for total health.

Spiritual needs

Since these needs are perhaps more subtle in nature and require of us a greater degree of self-awareness if we are to become fully alive to them, many of us may tend to neglect our soul needs. They are, however, extremely important in the context of our overall level of health.

The soul needs:

1) an *achievable* purpose
2) to recognise and express its *uniqueness*
3) to *grow* and evolve
4) a loving and nourishing social support group; to feel *connected*
5) the *freedom* to know and express itself fully
6) to feel it is *contributing* in some way to the Greater Plan
7) to feel *secure*.

❁   **Exercise: looking at different areas of your life to see if your soul needs are being met.**

Take the areas of your life listed below (adding any others you like!). How many of the seven soul needs listed above are satisfied in each situation? (Place a tick under the relevant number.)

	0	1	2	3	4	5	6	7
Your major partnership	…	…	…	…	…	…	…	…
Your work	…	…	…	…	…	…	…	…
Your role as parent	…	…	…	…	…	…	…	…
Your role as child	…	…	…	…	…	…	…	…
Your role as sibling	…	…	…	…	…	…	…	…
Your social life	…	…	…	…	…	…	…	…

While respecting and honouring our individuality, at a soul level each of us needs to see ourselves as part of all life forms within this Earth, part of the planet, the solar system, the Universe and hence of our Creator. In truth, total health can be achieved only when all these aspects are in health or Whole.

Ultimately we ALL seek PEACE OF MIND.

A visualisation for health

An important aspect of this visualisation, which introduces **Inner Dialogue with the Body**, is the help it gives you to activate your **Inner Healer**. This complements any other form of therapy, including orthodox medicine. Our innate healing powers make their presence known through the **Intuition**. They help us to choose the most appropriate form of treatment at that moment, and in so doing engage the powerful intelligence of both body and mind to bring us to a state of harmony.

Allow yourself plenty of time; make sure you will not be interrupted or disturbed by family, visitors, pets or telephone. These simple steps will offer you the opportunity to gain as much as possible from the exercise.

This is an imagery exercise; have paper and coloured pens or pencils to hand so you can make a record of your experience.

❀ ONCE you are in a comfortable position, allow yourself to relax by taking a few deep, slow breaths. As you breathe out, allow any cares or tension to be carried away on the breath. Imagine them simply floating away ...

❁ AS before this is an opportunity to connect with your Inner Healer; have an awareness of the nature of that connection.

❁ IT may be a thought or there may be a visual dimension such as an image, picture, shape or colour appearing on your 'inner screen'. When you feel in touch with the healing power within, take the awareness to any part of your body where there is disharmony, pain or disease.

IF YOUR BODY IS HEALTHY, YOU MAY PREFER TO TAKE YOUR AWARENESS TO SOMETHING ELSE YOU WISH TO HEAL — PERHAPS AN EMOTIONAL STATE OR AN ATTITUDE YOU FIND UNACCEPTABLE. YOU MAY PREFER TO WORK WITH A DISEASE FROM THE PAST WHICH IS NOT FULLY UNDERSTOOD.

❁ ASK your Inner Healer for a picture or image which represents or expresses the aspect of yourself in disharmony, pain or discomfort.

TRY NOT TO BE TOO ANATOMICAL; SEE THE PICTURE AS SOMETHING ABSTRACT, WHICH COULD BE DRAWN ON PAPER.

ALLOW THE FIRST IMAGE TO BE THE 'RIGHT' ONE. DON'T CHANGE IT, EVEN IF IT IS UNCOMFORTABLE TO SEE!

❁ IF you were to hang the picture in a gallery, what title would you give it?

❁ IF this picture could talk to you, what would it say? What is its message for you?

❋ IN the knowledge that the picture would appear only to help you in a healing process, ask your Inner Healer what is to be learned through this experience or what is the opportunity of this illness or discomfort.

ANOTHER WAY OF LOOKING AT THIS IS TO BECOME AWARE OF WHAT HAS CHANGED IN YOUR LIFE — IN A POSITIVE SENSE — SINCE THE PAIN OR DISHARMONY BEGAN.

❋ HAVE a sense of what you will do when the disharmony is no longer present.

❋ RETURNING to your picture or image, open yourself to the possibility that you can transform the image using your creative imagination or visualisation skills.

❋ ALLOW the image to transform until it represents harmony, health and wholeness in that organ, emotion or attitude. Be aware of the differences between the original image, and the transformed one.

❋ ONCE you feel complete with the process, gently allow your awareness to return to the space in which you chose to work, bringing with you the information you received.

NOW IT'S TIME FOR THE FINAL STEP IN THE PROCESS — AND IT'S AN IMPORTANT ONE. RECORD YOUR EXPERIENCE IN DRAWINGS, ADDING WORDS WHEREVER APPROPRIATE, AND IF POSSIBLE SHARE THEM WITH A FRIEND OR THERAPIST SO YOU CAN GAIN MAXIMUM BENEFIT FROM THE EXERCISE.

Illness as messenger

'*When we get the symptoms of a cold,*' says AIDS patient
George Melton, '*we run down to the drugstore to get
something to suppress them so we can go back to the
behaviour that gave us the cold in the first place ... Stop
trying to kill the messenger, and listen to the message.*'

The language of disease

As a starting point in exploring what those precious 'messages' maybe,
we should not overlook clues offered by the language we use. If the
following examples seem obvious, stop for a moment to think about
them. In your experience, is there any validity in making these simple
connections?

Symptom	Signifying?
Stomach pain	Difficulty in '**stomaching**' or digesting something? Have you taken on too much?
Bronchial catarrh	Need to '**get something off your chest**'?
A lump in the throat	Finding something **difficult to swallow** – or express?
Neck pain	Is someone or something a '**pain in the neck**'?

Shingles	Someone '**getting on your nerves**'?
Nausea	Are you '**sick of something – or someone**'?
Short sight	Inability or reluctance to '**look further ahead – or at the bigger picture**'?

 Working from this perspective, perhaps you can see other examples in your own life. If so, write them down.

....
....
....
....
....

The opportunities offered

To gain a deeper appreciation of the true meaning and significance of illness, we need to look at some of the main functions illness can perform. As you read this section, it may be illuminating to get a sense of which – if any – are relevant either to your own experience or your experience of others.

As you do so, it is important to suspend judgement. This is not about making people feel guilty, nor ascribing blame or shame. It is about gaining a greater understanding of ourselves and other human beings in a spirit of caring and compassion.

Gaining increased understanding is also important inasmuch as *conscious awareness of the experience of illness greatly enhances the healing process.* For this to happen, however, consciousness needs to be at a cellular rather than an intellectual level. *It is not enough to know the theory - you need to experience an 'Ah-ha!' deep in your being.*

It is also worth bearing in mind that invariably dis-ease or disharmony is present at an intellectual or emotional level before it manifests in the body. We can choose to deal with the situation at those levels, or, like most human beings, wait until we have physical evidence - i.e. when we are stopped in our tracks - before we take the appropriate remedial action.

Have the courage to take a bird's eye view of your own illnesses, past or present, and ask yourself 'What is the opportunity of the illness?'

Illness can be ...

1 ... A prime mover for transition

Illness can prevent the individual from moving along their old path. Although some part of them knows their present path is not the right one, sometimes it is easier or more comfortable not to hear. It is then left to their body to force them to listen. Once the illness has been treated, any attempt to return to the old path is likely to result in recurrence.

Good examples are Chronic Fatigue Syndrome or ME, which tend to manifest when the soul and the personality are following two entirely separate paths, and the time has come to combine forces. The very symptoms of ME such as tiredness, aching muscles and disturbed body rhythms reflect the disassociation between these two great masters of our body.

 Take a few moments to pause and consider this question:

Do you have any sense that the path you are currently following may not be the right one for you?

If the answer is 'yes' – and for many of us it is – the way to retain your health and well-being is first to acknowledge the truth, then to discover what you want out of life, and finally make the changes necessary to achieve this.

 Make a list of the things you would most like to do if you knew planet Earth would cease to exist in six months. What would you change in your life?

....

....

....

....

....

....

....

....

2 ... A 'voice'

For some people there are times when it is so hard to put a feeling into words that their Physical Body acts as 'spokesperson' – communicating through sickness or disease. A common instance is *acute arthritis*, which prevents certain activities around which there is underlying resentment. Daring to speak the appropriate words can facilitate remarkable levels of cure; failure to speak them can result in the condition continuing.

Speaking your truth – especially when it involves expressing anger or resentment – can be a truly daunting proposition. If you find yourself in this position, have you considered the possibility of saying what needs to be said not with the energy of the underlying emotion, but simply owning the feeling? There is a world of difference between: 'You make me so angry ...' and 'I feel really angry about ...'

If you find 'speaking your truth' in a particular situation is very challenging, have you considered alternative methods of having your say, which may be less difficult or threatening?

One very good one is to write a letter to the person or the people involved. Allow yourself complete freedom to put into words the feelings you experience.

When you are satisfied you have expressed yourself as fully and powerfully as you wish, see what you would really like to do with your letter. You don't have to send it – although you may wish to do so. Some people find it helpful to destroy their letter, perhaps by burning, letting go of any uncomfortable feelings relating to its contents or the people to whom it is addressed, and sending their thoughts through the ether with love.

3 ... The soul's message

In these instances, disease is the way in which unexpressed disharmony on the emotional level gains expression through the Physical Body. Disease is a message from the soul signifying change is required.

The disease actually contains clues to the nature of the change required, and when it has been made. Aching shoulders, for example, may well indicate the sufferer is 'carrying too great a burden of responsibility' (often for other people). Once that load has been lightened, the shoulder condition will begin to get better.

4 ... Avoidance

Illness may be a way of seeking to avoid a soul change which is imminent. A clue to help you recognise this situation is hearing the words (maybe from your own mouth): 'I'd love to, but ...' A typical example is the older person who experiences a frequent need to pass water (which relates to insecurity and fear of being out of control). This apparent 'problem' in fact allows them to stay at home, thus avoiding potentially threatening situations.

As this example illustrates, becoming aware of how we ourselves are acting and speaking can be very illuminating. Listen to the phraseology you use; it will often tell you what you 'really want to do', 'would love to do', or 'given the chance would do'. Let phrases like that pop up and grab your attention – practise listening to the part of you expressing desire, and the part which is finding reasons why it cannot be.

> ❀ **List phrases you use when you are:**
>
> - tired ....
>   ....
> - happy ....
>   ....
> - in pain ....
>   ....
> - worried ....
>   ....
> - excited ....
>   ....
> - angry ....
>   ....

5 ... *A provider of secondary gain*

This is often imagined to be one of the commonest causes of illness by onlookers, but is in fact quite unusual. Secondary gain is experienced when an individual, rather than release their illness and move forward, stays in pain and suffering in order to satisfy the desires of the personality.

This frequently has a manipulative or attention-seeking dimension, the sufferer using their condition to control another (often a partner or close family member) or others. Back pain, for example, may be used to attract sympathy, and for a few days proves successful. When the pain subsides and the carers drift back to their old preoccupations, guess what? Yes – the pain returns!

Remember this is invariably an unconscious process. It is common amongst children, for whom becoming 'ill' or perhaps having 'accidents' is the only way they know to get the attention of their parents. Do you have some recollection of using illness in this way as a tool?

6 ... The means of punishing others

Sad to say, illness can be used as a kind of 'stick' with which to beat other people. Even though the intention is on a subconscious level, the effect can be profound, and reveals issues which are unresolved or unexpressed. The unconscious thought behind the action is: 'I'll show them!' In instances of illness being used in this way, the 'patient' may be prepared to go to great lengths, enduring intense and prolonged pain and perhaps even risking death to achieve the desired level of punishment.

7 ... A teacher for the soul

A moving illustration of illness perceived by the sufferer as an aid for the soul to learn about life on another level is provided by a book entitled *A Child of Eternity*. The author, now a young woman, describes being conscious of cutting off her nutrition whilst in the womb, with the result that she was born autistic. Her 'soul challenge', she believes, is to learn to communicate without screaming and shouting. This is being realised for, using a computer, she now writes books which are an inspiration to others.

Having a family member who suffers from a condition like autism presents enormous challenges for others in the group. It may be of help to consider the possibility that for the individual with the condition, the experience is necessary for their 'soul growth' and development.

8 ... A gift to growth and healing for others

This aspect of illness is most frequently seen in the case of children who are sick, when their condition leads to the healing and soul growth of the family or those who care for them in hospital.

People often ask why young children should have to suffer traumatic illnesses. While it remains distressing for their family to witness their suffering, it may help to acknowledge the possibility that there is nothing 'chance' about disease, and in such cases it may be part of the soul's path.

We should also be mindful of the fact that a child's view of life differs from that of an adult; children live in the moment rather than being driven by long-term expectations.

There is the lovely story of a little boy of three saying to his mother: 'Mummy, I was in someone else's tummy before I was in yours – but there was another baby in there, and it kicked me out!' A tale of a twin pregnancy for which some mother may still grieve ... out of the mouths of babes!

9 ... A karmic healer

Disease can fulfil this role on either a personal or global level. In the first case, it may manifest when an individual experiences a deeper karmic illness which is brought to the surface at the same age as a strong emotion which became locked into their energy field during a past life. On a wider level, a group may manifest a planetary karmic illness, perhaps as part of the evolutionary cycle of Mother Earth. There are so many things in Heaven and Earth which defy rational explanation.

10 ... Defence through helplessness

Some diseases lead to a state of helplessness – most obviously in the case of chronic pain. This state can be so all encompassing that the sufferer has great difficulty in recognising they have a role to play in their own healing – let alone what the nature of that role may be.

11 ... An initiation

Illness – especially when serious – can represent a process of initiation for an individual to pass from one phase of life to the next. In this context, we are looking beyond the perspective of a single earthly existence being all there is of 'life', and that illness may lead to physical – although not spiritual – death. We all have to die from something!

Nothing happens by chance, and illness is often the only way to stop us in our tracks when nothing else has worked. Listen within and clear the channel for a healthy and happy life.

In instances of 'disease as initiation' it is important to remember that death is not 'failure'. Equally, not all 'healing' results in a continuation of physical life. Healing may be powerful and effective in terms of allowing an individual to pass from one plane to another.

Voice dialogue with the body

This exercise is designed to enable you to dialogue directly with your body, drawing upon your innate 'body wisdom'. You can use it whenever you wish to discover more about the deeper meaning of a physical symptom.

Voice dialogue, whilst essentially very simple, is powerful and transformational. First find a partner who will take the role of facilitator. Their job is to ask questions of whatever part of your body may hold the information you need to hear.

(The dialogue may need to be with a sub-personality rather than an organ or limb – and the process is identical.

For simplicity, in the following guidelines, reference is made to the Physical Body only.)

You, meanwhile, take the role of that part of the body, and become its spokesperson.

Before beginning, read the next section together. Once you are both clear about the process, it can flow easily, and without interruption.

Allow the exercise as much time as possible — 15–20 minutes is ideal. Comfort is important, whether you choose to sit or lie down. Your partner may find it useful to take notes during the process, so sitting may be preferable for them. Being fairly close together makes hearing easy — having to ask the other person to repeat what they have said tends to disturb the flow.

✾ ONCE you have made yourself comfortable, an ideal way to begin is to spend a few moments in silence, perhaps using relaxing breaths, each person tuning in to their 'Inner Healer' for guidance and help during the process. Create a 'sacred space' between you, honouring one another.

✾ WHEN they are ready, the facilitator begins by asking you for some symptom, pain or illness about which you would like more information in terms of its purpose, meaning or message. When you have chosen one, they will ask for a brief history of the chosen issue, to provide the necessary background.

✾ THE process now becomes a dialogue between the part of your body manifesting disharmony and the facilitator. Let yourself identify with that part and allow it to give the answers through your voice.

❁ IT is important to show respect for the relevant part of the body by inviting it to dialogue, so the process might typically continue something like this:

FACILITATOR: 'Hello, David's knee. Are you
                       happy to talk to me?'

YOURSELF: 'This is David's knee. Yes, that's
                       fine.'

FACILITATOR: 'I understand you've been giving
                       David some problems. I know you
                       only want to help him, so will you
                       tell me what is the special role you
                       play in his life. Why were you
                       chosen to express disharmony?'

YOURSELF: 'My role in David's life is to help
                       him become aware of ...'

FACILITATOR: 'Thank you. If he heard this, would
                       it be enough, or is there anything
                       else he needs to know ...?'

❁ DIALOGUE of this kind continues until the facilitator is confident they have received and understood the body's message. This may involve similar dialogue with another, different part of the body (or another sub-personality), always asking permission to dialogue with the new area offered.

❁ WHEN the facilitator feels they have received all relevant information, it is important to leave the person feeling strong. If distress has been caused, they should ask the person to connect with a part of the body which is strong, and ask for help from that part for the whole person.

❁ FINALLY, they may like to ask the body if it feels the process is complete. If it is, it remains only for the facilitator to acknowledge those parts of the body which have contributed by thanking them, after which the exercise may be drawn gently to a close.

Some further points which you may find valuable:

- Each different part of you, whether physical or mental, will have its own individual stance and way of speaking. You may wish to take on that stance when speaking from the different parts of the body, thereby gaining increased insight and benefit from the work.

- Ultimately, the body is seeking to regain a state of harmony and balance. The illness is not the enemy but, on the contrary, a messenger carrying information about the requisite healing process. Hear the message as coming from a friend.

- The body may have a sense of the time which will be required to allow healing to take place. Ask when 'David' will be well again.

- It is recommended the facilitator should make a brief record of the process. A great deal of information may be imparted, and notes help to refresh the memory so that further discussion and exploration can take place where appropriate.

Most of us perceive illness as something hostile and unfriendly rather than as a messenger bearing a special and precious gift. As a result, we have a tendency to 'shoot the messenger' rather than listen to what it has to tell us. This Chapter contains a variety of methods of 'tuning in' to whatever your body may be trying to communicate when you suffer disease. If you are interested in developing deeper understandings in this area, the following books are recommended:

Christine Page - *Frontiers of Health* - C W Daniel Company Ltd 1992

Louise L Hay - *You Can Heal Your Life* - Eden Grove Editions 1984

Thorwald Dethlefson & Rudiger Hahlke - *The Healing Power of Illness* - Element 1983

Stephen Levine - *Healing into Life and Death* - Gateway 1989

Caroline Myss - *Anatomy of the Spirit* - Bantam Books 1996

The Chakras

Auras, chakras and the subtle energy system

According to many Eastern traditions human beings, in addition to their familiar, tangible body, possess a **subtle energy** system. Consisting of a field of energy radiating from and surrounding their physical form, it is visible to some of those blessed with clairvoyant or psychic gifts. For such people the aura, and in particular the colours it contains, carries a wealth of information about the state of the individual's spiritual, mental, emotional and physical health.

As illustrated in the diagram below, the **aura** incorporates seven 'bodies' or expressions of the human spirit which are interconnecting fields of energy, each vibrating at a different rate. Shown below in decreasing order of vibrational rate, they are: the Divine Body, the Spiritual Body and the Soul Body (together forming the Higher Self) together with the Mental, Astral, Etheric and Physical Bodies (together forming the Personality or Lower Self).

Exploring auras ...

Many children see auras as colours surrounding people. Some retain this gift into adulthood as was the case with a friend of mine who, learning about auras for the first time on a self-awareness course, realised he had always been able to see ' pale shadows round people', but had never known what they were! Even if we do not see auras we often sense them in other ways.

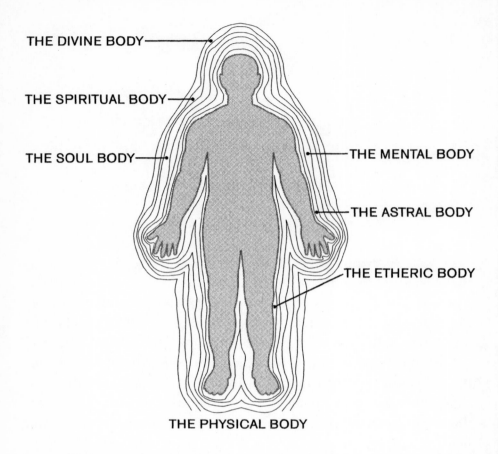

THE DIVINE BODY

THE SPIRITUAL BODY

THE SOUL BODY

THE MENTAL BODY

THE ASTRAL BODY

THE ETHERIC BODY

THE PHYSICAL BODY

You may recall the experience of entering a train, bus or room, and sensing that you were drawn to sit in a particular seat – near to or perhaps away from certain people. In such situations we are responding to our inner and outer senses to 'read another's aura' and see what feels in harmony with our own.

When we are in close proximity to others – perhaps in an aeroplane or a busy train – we draw our aura round us like a cloak. In other spaces, perhaps when we are 'performing or relating', our aura extends to touch those we wish to contact.

... through touch

For the following exercises you will need the aid of a friend.

✱ Exercise One

1   Begin by making contact, standing facing one another, your palms lightly touching theirs. Allow the energy to flow freely between you for a few moments.
2   Ask your friend to stand in a comfortable position, about four feet away.
3   Both of you raise your hands in front of you at chest height, palms towards the other.
4   Approach each other slowly, awareness focused on the palms of your hands.
5   As you get closer, see if you sense anything through your palms – perhaps a slight tingling, a change of temperature, or a feeling of resistance, as if you have encountered an invisible barrier. (Such sensations typically occur when the hands are 4–6 inches from the other person's.)
6   See how far apart you can move before you feel something different.

✱ Exercise Two

7   Now, using one hand (allow yourself to decide whether your left or right hand is more sensitive), see if you can 'feel' your friend's aura, moving round different parts of their body. What differences do you feel in different places?
8   Ask your friend whether they, too, experience changes in sensation as your hands pass around them. If so, ask them to describe it.
9   Experiment by changing roles and comparing what each of you experienced.

Chakras

Chakra is a Sanskrit word meaning 'wheel' or 'circle'. Those who see chakras describe them as circular in form, whirling as they draw forces and energies into the body. Chakras serve as 'conduits' or channels interconnecting the Physical Body with energies emanating from the subtle bodies which constitute the aura.

They are of vital importance, for they collate and distribute information coming in from the subtle bodies, and also relay feedback to them. By this process they enable the individual to maintain physical health while simultaneously growing and developing spiritually. In the words of David Tansley: *'These centres of force ... represent the seven levels of consciousness, and serve as points of entry to the inner worlds ...'*

There are seven primary chakras, positioned as shown below:

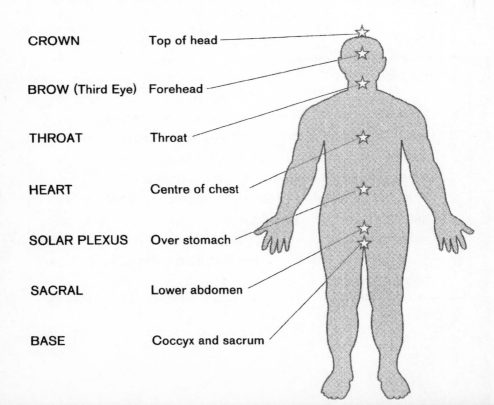

CROWN	Top of head
BROW (Third Eye)	Forehead
THROAT	Throat
HEART	Centre of chest
SOLAR PLEXUS	Over stomach
SACRAL	Lower abdomen
BASE	Coccyx and sacrum

Crown, Throat and Heart relate principally to the energies of the soul.

The role of the Brow or Third Eye is to act as intermediary between the soul and the personality (which is the vehicle for the soul's earthly journey).

Base, Sacral and Solar Plexus relate principally to the personality. (Full development of the three lower chakras is vital to ensure full expression of the soul's energies.)

How the chakras function

The seven principal chakras correspond to specific endocrine glands, and their function can be described as follows:

1
Energetic impulses entering each chakra from different subtle bodies intermingle until a combined force passes into the Physical Body via the Etheric

5
The response is fed into the chakra which transmits the energy into the subtle bodies, which assess the response, changing and sending a new impulse into the chakra

2
The energetic force activates the brain and the autonomic nervous system, leading to the stimulation of the endocrine gland to produce hormones

4
The effect of the hormones on the individual is fed back, via the bloodstream, to the originating glands where it is compared with the original impulse from the subtle bodies

3
These hormones are carried around the body via the bloodstream to target sites where the impulse from the subtle bodies manifests in action

This constant process illustrates how the function of the Physical Body is dependent on the activity of the chakras, which is in turn dependent on the energy of the subtle bodies.

We have touched on the nature of the chakras, the basic function they fulfil (which we shall examine in greater detail later in this Chapter), and how they work. Now you have an opportunity to connect with and experience your own chakra system.

Getting to know your chakras

This visualisation is designed to take you on a tour of your energy system, and learn more about it — through your own unique experience.

As with any visualisation exercise, remember the basics: allow plenty of time, choose a place in which to work where you will be comfortable and not interrupted. Have a notebook at hand for any record you may wish to make of the exercise when it is complete. Loosen any tight clothing, and either lie down or sit with both feet on the floor.

❀ TAKE a few good deep breaths. If you are aware of any stress or tension in your body, release it on the outbreath.

SOME PEOPLE LIKE TO IMAGINE THAT WHATEVER THEY ARE RELEASING IS PASSING THROUGH THE SOLES OF THEIR FEET, BEING ABSORBED INTO THE EARTH, AND TRANSFORMED.

✸ ASK your inner mind to be open to any information which will help you to grow and heal.

✸ GENTLY take your awareness to your base chakra. As you do so, be aware of the nature of the energy-flow through it.

IS THE FLOW THROUGH THE BASE CHAKRA EASY AND NATURAL, OR DO YOU HAVE A SENSE OF RESTRICTION OR BLOCKAGE?

✸ ALLOW your awareness to remain focused a little longer on your Base chakra. Is your sense of the energy-flow accompanied by an image or a physical sensation?

ALLOW AWARENESS OF YOUR RESPONSE AT ANY LEVEL. IF YOU EXPERIENCE A PICTURE, BODY SENSATION, CHANGE IN BREATHING PATTERN, THOUGHTS OR EMOTION, STORE IT SAFELY IN YOUR MEMORY SO YOU CAN RECALL IT AT THE END OF THE PROCESS.

IF YOU WISH YOU CAN MAKE A NOTE AFTER EACH CHAKRA, BUT TRY TO REMAIN IN A QUIET STATE AS YOU WRITE OR DRAW.

✸ WHEN you feel complete with your Base chakra, allow a space during which to clear your thoughts and centre yourself.

THE 'CLEARING PROCESS' ALLOWS YOU TO COMPLETE WITH ONE CHAKRA BEFORE ATTENDING TO THE NEXT ONE WITH AN OPEN MIND.

✸ THIS done, transfer awareness to your Sacral chakra, and repeat the process detailed above.

✸ ALLOWING as much time as you need for each one, use this method to explore your • Solar Plexus chakra • Heart chakra • Throat chakra • Brow chakra • Crown chakra.

DURING THIS PROCESS YOU ARE OPENING YOURSELF TO SUBTLE
AND DELICATE RESPONSES FROM YOUR PHYSICAL BODY, SENSES,
EMOTIONS AND IMAGINATION. IT IS ALSO AN EXPERIENCE TO
SAVOUR AND **ENJOY**!

❃ BEFORE 'departing' from your energy system, take time to ensure leaving it in a state of peace and balance. One way of doing this is to imagine each chakra closing gently like a flower when your work with it is complete.

SOME PEOPLE 'CLOSE DOWN' THEIR CHAKRAS USING LIGHT —
PERHAPS COLOURED LIGHT. TRUST THAT WHATEVER METHOD
YOU ARE GUIDED TO USE IS THE RIGHT ONE FOR YOU.

❃ WHEN you have completed the exercise, take as much time as you need to return to the physical space from which you undertook your 'Chakra Tour'.

THE FINAL, IMPORTANT STEP IS TO RECORD ANY ASPECT OF THE
EXPERIENCE — IT MAY BE AN IMAGE, EMOTION OR SENSATION —
WHICH HOLDS SIGNIFICANCE FOR YOU.

❃ WHEN you feel fully back in your body, open your eyes …

IN THE SECTION WHICH FOLLOWS, YOU WILL FIND SUGGESTIONS
REGARDING THE MEANING OF THE CHAKRAS WHICH MAY PROVIDE
YOU WITH VALUABLE INSIGHTS.

IT CAN BE WONDERFUL TO SHARE YOUR FINDINGS WITH ANOTHER PERSON,
RECEIVING THEIR NON-JUDGEMENTAL THOUGHTS AND WISDOM.

Chakras and human development

As human beings mature, we achieve a more refined sense of our personal and spiritual power. The chakras are of special significance in this process, since *each chakra represents a specific spiritual 'life-lesson'* on our path. As we master those lessons, we move along that path, steadily increasing our spiritual awareness.

The challenges relating to each chakra are:

Base: Lessons relating to the material world, basic security and a sense of belonging.

Sacral: Sexuality, relationships, dependency/independence and nurturing.

Solar Plexus: Ego, storage of emotions, desires and self-esteem.

Heart: Forgiveness, compassion and unconditional love.

Throat: Will, logic, self-expression and creativity.

Brow: Intuition, wisdom, insight and self-responsibility.

Crown: Spirituality, purpose and global consciousness.

The way we choose to respond (or not respond!) to such challenges has a direct influence on our physical health. This understanding is based on the fact that:

If we decline to accept responsibility, and ignore the challenges we are offered, their energy can lead to the manifestation of disease in the mind or body as a way of correcting the imbalance.

It can also manifest in non-physical forms like the breakdown of a relationship or loss of a job.

Let us assume, for example, the lessons we need to learn in our present incarnation relate to issues round the material world and our connection to it. If we choose to ignore rather than respond to them, we are more likely to manifest the physical illnesses primarily associated with the Base chakra. These include: constipation, piles, colitis, kidney stones, impotence and hypertension.

For those suffering from complaints like these, beginning to work on the underlying issues can produce startling results in terms of healing the physical disease.

Chakras and body language ...

For some people, relating to chakras on a theoretical, conceptual level presents difficulties. They may find it more natural to connect with them through the medium of practical, 'every day' experience. Body language, which is largely 'driven' by our energy system, provides an excellent opportunity to do precisely this.

Body language	**Which may signify someone is ...**
1) Hand held to heart	Responding to 'heart-felt' emotions such as the fear of being hurt
2) Hand placed across throat	Finding difficulty in expressing themselves
3) Hand on the brow	Having to deal with a 'critical voice'
4) Hands linked across solar plexus	Protecting themselves against uncomfortable emotions or 'gut feelings'
5) Intertwined legs	Feeling sexually vulnerable

... and how this relates to the chakras:

1   This gesture often indicates that the person is feeling vulnerable in relation to their need to be loved and accepted. At some level, they fear those needs will not be met; the instinctive body response is to protect or cover the Heart chakra.

2   From the list on the previous page, you will remember the Throat chakra corresponds to will and self-expression. We often cover the throat when we are aware there is something we need to express, but for some reason – often fear – we feel unable to do so.

3   One of several challenges relating to the Brow chakra is that of *distinguishing our own inner truth and wisdom* from what we have been *told* is true. A hand pressed to the brow often indicates conflict or confusion between the two.

4   The Solar Plexus is our personal power centre. Folding our hands across it may signal that, consciously or unconsciously, we are feeling that our personal power is threatened – perhaps by energy we are picking up from someone else, or something they are saying.

5   Legs wound round one another indicate an unconscious need to protect the Base chakra, which is related to the 'power' side of sexuality, and is susceptible to vulnerability.

Chakras and health

You now have all the information necessary to complete a simple but illuminating exercise. Bringing together the understandings offered so far in this Chapter, it will enable you to relate to your past medical history, to the state of your energy system, and to the nature of your unique personal challenges.

What your medical history tells you ...

❀ **Look down the following list of the more common ailments, illnesses and diseases. Ring the numbers of those from which you are currently suffering or have suffered in the past:**

1 **Panic attack**	16 Cancer
2 **Kidney stone**	17 ME, chronic fatigue
3 **Hypertension**	syndrome
4 **Hypotension**	18 Auto-immune illnesses
5 **Osteoarthritis of the**	19 **Tinnitus**
hips	20 **Sore throat**
6 **Cystitis**	21 **Breathing problems**
7 Fibroids	22 **Thyroid problems**
8 Prostate disease	23 **Gum disorders**
9 Irritable bowel disease	24 **Deafness**
10 Lower back pain	25 Migraine
11 **Ulcers (duodenal or**	26 Tension headaches
gastric)	27 Glaucoma
12 **Diabetes**	28 Learning difficulties
13 **Anorexia**	29 Problems with vision
14 **Gall stones**	30 **Epilepsy**
15 Heart disease or	31 **Alzheimer's**
malfunction	32 **Depression**

... *about your energy system*

30–32 Indicate your life challenges may well lie in the areas of your spiritual or mystical connections, or sense of purpose. (Crown chakra.)

25–29 Problems of this nature in the energy system suggest as their underlying cause fear of relying on inner guidance, failure to see the larger picture, unwillingness to face one's own fears, or inability to focus on what is important. (Brow chakra.)

19–24 You may be struggling emotionally and mentally with lessons relating to learning the nature of the power of choice, or unwillingness to let go, trust and allow yourself to express fully who you are. (Throat chakra.)

15–18 All these illnesses relate to the freedom with which we are able to open our hearts, allow our emotional responses to flow, and enjoy life. (Heart chakra.)

11–14 Poor self-esteem, need for approval, fear of rejection and sensitivity to criticism are just four of the powerful issues with which sufferers from these conditions may be struggling. (Solar Plexus chakra.)

7–10 Susceptibility to these disorders suggests difficulty with relationships, fear of vulnerability, and feeling unsupported. (Sacral chakra.)

1–6 Here, issues round the 'will to be' are highlighted. These may include deep-seated fears around survival, fears of abandonment or rejection, and fear of losing control. (Base chakra.)

Your medical history provides a great deal of valuable information about your energy system since, as we have already seen, the two are interdependent. Equally revealing – and equally helpful in seeing where healing work may most usefully be directed – is information supplied by your character structure. This is the way you live your life – the way in which you respond to being in the world and the challenges you meet in your everyday existence.

Studying the traits listed below, you may well recognise some as being relevant to you. If you do, resist the impulse to put a judgement on them – to see them as good, bad, positive or negative. If, for example, you identify with a need to 'stay in control', it is easy to fall into the trap of feeling there is something bad or wrong about it. In fact, the ability to remain in control is extremely valuable in certain areas of our life, whereas in others it may equally limit and restrict us. The key is not the trait itself but our own level of awareness about what we are doing; whether it is a 'knee-jerk response' or a conscious choice.

The purpose in acknowledging these traits is to use them as guides for the work of our Inner Healer – the part of ourself which knows how to heal old hurts and wounds, and helps us reclaim those parts of ourselves with which we may have lost touch on our journey through life. A powerful process to begin that healing process is detailed after the exercise.

How personality traits relate to chakras

Take your time to look at the lists which follow. Engage with the questions from a place of inner knowing and awareness. You may find your instant response to some questions is a very quick: 'Oh no – that's not me at all!' And you may be right. Or ... there may be a resistance to acknowledging this part of yourself. Allow a few moments in case that instant rejection wants to become ... 'Well, maybe it *is* true. Maybe that's the way I am, sometimes.'

And don't stop the process when you have found a chakra which you recognise needs some Tender Loving Care. There will probably be several, and it may be true for all!

❀		Yes	No
	Has zest and enthusiasm faded from your life?	....	....
	Do you ever feel life has lost its purpose?	....	....
	Are you 'off the tracks' – perhaps even experiencing the 'dark night of the soul'?	....	....
	Are you devoid of emotion, working almost exclusively through intellect?	....	....
	Are you a day-dreamer, sometimes living in a fantasy world?	....	....

If you recognise yourself, there is healing work to be done on your Crown chakra.

❋ Do you feel responsible for other people (while perhaps failing to acknowledge your own needs)?

Do you feel 'driven' rather than feeling you are 'in the driving seat'?

Are you highly conscientious, over-serious and over-responsible?

Do you find it difficult to be spontaneous – to play?

Are you a martyr to a cause?

Do you feel confused, disorientated and unsure of your direction?

Are you a *black and white* person, with no shades of grey?

Do you have a tendency to judge rather than observe with compassion?

Yes   No

The relationship of these characteristics is with the Brow chakra (or Third Eye).

❋ Although your mind is full of thoughts and ideas, is there too little action in your life?

Does your creativity feel blocked?

Are you highly analytical?

Are you frightened of failure, taking risks, or taking responsibility?

Do you believe the world 'out there' is dangerous or even hostile?

Do you have a fear of speaking out because of the possible consequences?

Do you find you constantly make excuses when challenged to move forward or change?

Yes   No

These are some of the ways blockage in the energy flow through your Throat chakra may make itself felt.

❀ Do you feel lonely or an outsider – even in a crowd?   **Yes** .... **No** ....

Do you find yourself ruled by *SMOG – Should, Must, Ought* and *Got to*?   ....

Are you dissatisfied with your job or your life, and feel there is no way out?   ....

Do you try desperately to avoid conflict, even when feeling angry inside?   ....

Do you find it difficult to love *all* of yourself?   ....

Do you identify with the world purely by what you do and your role in society?   ....

Have you lost your sense of 'I'?   ....

Are these your personality traits? They relate to the Heart chakra.

❀ Do you ever feel unloved or under-valued?   **Yes** **No**

Are you the kind who 'waves a banner' – are you determined and dogmatic?   ....

Are you uncomplaining, sometimes usurped in a relationship?   ....

Are you *over*-sensitive to the feelings of other people?   ....

Do you fear the world 'out there'?   ....

Do you find it hard to say 'no!' to people?   ....

Do you care for others but harbour secret resentment as a result?   ....

Do you ever do things with a smile yet feel resentful underneath?   ....

Do you sense atmospheres – of places and people?   ....

Do you desperately need approval?   ....

Do you need to be needed or liked?   ....

Are you a '*pleaser*'?   ....

These characteristics suggest work on healing the Solar Plexus.

✻ Do you care for and nurture others, but leave no space for your needs?	Yes	No
Are you a *great* giver but a *lousy* receiver?	....	....
Do you feel overwhelmed by the demands of others, yet fail to speak out?	....	....
Are you fiercely independent, fearful of becoming vulnerable?	....	....
Do you ever feel used or abused?	....	....
Have you ever planted your 'seed of creativity' and been disappointed it failed to grow?	....	....
Do you feel unsupported by money or by other people?	....	....

All of the above are Sacral chakra issues.

✻ Do you have a need to stay 'in control' of yourself, or others?	Yes	No
Are you secretive?	....	....
Are you wary, alert, unable to rest?	....	....
Are you afraid of criticism?	....	....
Are you 'stiff' or 'rigid' in body or mind?	....	....
Do you fear to walk your own path, yet always ready to help others do it?	....	....
Are you holding on to past fears or grievances?	....	....
Are you a perfectionist, critical or obsessive?	....	....
Is the intimacy of sexual intercourse attended by fear or embarrassment?	....	....
Are others 'never quite good enough'?	....	....

Answering 'yes' to any of these questions indicates the Base chakra
may need healing work.

Don't panic if you find you said 'yes' to a lot of the questions! Awareness signals the start of healing, and this exercise will help that process ...

Balancing the chakras

You will require a little additional information on chakras in order to carry out this exercise. First, you need to be familiar with the colours which relate to each chakra.

Crown	Violet
Brow	Indigo
Throat	Blue
Heart	Green
Solar Plexus	Yellow
Sacral	Orange
Base	Red

Some people find it helpful when doing a visualisation involving chakras to have an idea of what they look like. One of the forms described by clairvoyants with the gift of seeing energy fields is of each chakra as an elongated horn or funnel, curving up slightly from the front of the body to the back.

The following exercise is for cleansing and balancing chakras. This is achieved by drawing a stream of sparkling, coloured light through each chakra in turn, using the colours listed above.

Begin by working on each chakra in turn. When you repeat the exercise, you may find it feels right to focus on one chakra only, or several. In work of this nature, remember: **There is no right and wrong. There is only what you feel is appropriate for you, at this particular moment.**

Working to heal elements of our energy system is sensitive and delicate work. Give it the respect it deserves; allow plenty of time and space. Space means finding a physical location where you feel comfortable, and making sure you will be undisturbed for as long as you need.

To save having to refer to the colour list, you may find it helpful before starting the exercise to familiarise yourself with the colours which relate to each chakra, remembering that they are the colours of the rainbow, progressing from red to violet.

❀ BEGIN by focusing on your breathing, employing it as the vehicle to release any stress or tension in your body. Take several deep breaths, in through the nose and out through the mouth. You may find it helpful to make a sound as you exhale.

❀ ONCE you feel relaxed, allow your awareness to focus on the Base chakra. You may find it helpful to let a picture of it form in your mind.

> SOME PEOPLE REPORT PHYSICAL SENSATIONS SUCH AS PRESSURE OR TINGLING IN THE RELEVANT AREA OF THE BODY, BUT IF THIS IS NOT YOUR EXPERIENCE, DON'T WORRY. IT MAY DEVELOP OVER TIME AS YOU REPEAT THE EXERCISE, BUT IT IS NOT REQUIRED FOR THE EXERCISE TO BE EFFECTIVE.

❀ ONCE you have an awareness of the Base chakra, have a sense of a ball of red light suspended in the air a few inches in front of it. (In the case of the Crown chakra, above the top of your head.) Take time to study the ball of light. Become aware of how bright it is, whether it is still or swirling. Is it 'solid', or sparkling and dancing?

❀ WHEN you are ready, use your in-breath to draw the ball of light into your chakra. You may find all the light passes into the chakra in one breath, or you may find it takes several breaths. On the out-breath, imagine any negative energy held in the chakra passing out through the soles of your feet, being absorbed into the earth and transformed.

EXHALING 'DEBRIS' WHICH MAY HAVE ACCUMULATED AND BLOCKED YOUR ENERGY SYSTEM IS AN IMPORTANT PART OF THE CLEANSING PROCESS.

❀ SEE if you have a sense of what happens to the light once it has passed through the chakra. Does it stay in your body? If so, in one particular area, or does it spread throughout your body? If you enjoyed drawing light through the chakra, why not repeat the process?

THIS IS YOUR PROCESS – PLAY WITH IT, ENJOY IT! GIVE YOURSELF PERMISSION TO DRAW IN LIGHT AS MANY TIMES AS YOU WISH, UNTIL YOU FEEL THAT CHAKRA'S NEED FOR LIGHT AT THIS MOMENT IS SATISFIED.

❀ ONCE you are complete with the Base chakra, pass on to the others in ascending order, repeating the process, using the appropriate colours.

❀ WHEN you have completed the process, allow a few moments to focus your attention on the flow of energy from the Crown down to the Base. Is the flow even, and do the chakras feel aligned, and healthy?

❀ WHEN we have focused on the chakras, it is important to return them to a state connected to outside reality. Some people like to surround

themselves with light; white, golden or perhaps rainbow
hued. Others ask for the support of their angel, or a
guide.

✸ ONCE this final stage is complete, allow your
awareness to return once more to everyday reality. Take
as much time as you need to accomplish this – rushing
off prematurely risks your being 'spaced out', or not
fully connected to that reality.

FINALLY, MAKE A NOTE OF ANYTHING YOU WISH TO RECORD ABOUT THE
EXPERIENCE. AS YOU PRACTISE WORK AT THIS LEVEL IT IS INTERESTING TO
NOTICE DEVELOPMENT OF YOUR CONSCIOUSNESS AND CHANGES IN THE
STATE OF YOUR CHAKRAS. IT IS ALSO POSSIBLE YOU MAY WISH TO DISCUSS
YOUR EXPERIENCE IN ENERGY WORK WITH A THERAPIST, OR SOMEONE ELSE
WITH THE SKILLS TO HELP YOU RECOGNISE ITS FULL SIGNIFICANCE.

Affirmations and the chakras

Louise Hay calls the use of affirmations *'reprogramming old tapes'*.
Affirmations can be described as messages we send to our subconscious
about beliefs and understandings on which we choose to base our
thoughts and actions. All too often, as a result of our life experience
we have taken on a set of deep-seated beliefs which are negative, and
therefore do not serve us. Using positive affirmations, we can replace
those beliefs with new ones which reflect a true picture of our world
as we want it to be from the depth of our soul, rather than the old,
distorted one.

Taking Base chakra issues as an example, the old picture might
have been along the lines of: 'I feel insecure about my place on the
planet, and I fear for my survival.' A positive affirmation offering a
contrasting perception, and the basis for a very different approach to

life, might be: 'I am fully aware of my position on this Earth, and know that my basic needs will always be met.'

Taking a minute or two to use the affirmations most relevant to yourself, especially at the end of meditation, can be a potent force for personal growth and development.

Crown
Self-knowing
'I am fully conscious of, and open to, the will of my Higher Mind.'

Third Eye
Self-responsibility
'I take full responsibility for my thoughts, words and actions.'

Throat
Self-expression
'I am willing to express my true self, and hence fully participate in my own creation.'

Heart
Self-love
'I love myself and others unconditionally, both in the giving and the receiving.'

Solar Plexus
Self-worth
'I am worthy to live my life to the fullest without fear or guilt, listening only to my own inner voice.'

Sacral
Self-respect
'I will respect my needs and the needs of others in any relationship, and will act accordingly.'

Base
Self-awareness
'I am fully aware of my position on this Earth, and know that my basic needs will always be met.'

Further reading

If this Chapter has stimulated your interest in the subject, here are some books which offer additional perspectives and understandings:

Christine Page – *Frontiers of Health* – C W Daniel Company Ltd 1992
Caroline Myss – *Anatomy of the Spirit* – Bantam Books 1996
David Tansley – *The Raiment of Light* – Arkana 1983
              – *Ray Paths and Chakra Gateways* – C W Daniel
              Company Ltd 1985

Colour Healing

'We can eat, drink, breathe, visualise and dance colour.'
LILIAN VERNER BONDS

Physical science tells us light is radiant energy which travels through space at 186,000 miles per second in the form of both waves and particles. Light vibrates at a variety of wavelengths and frequencies and of those colours visible to the human eye, red has the longest wavelength and violet the shortest.

Perhaps more significant in the context of healing is the understanding that the organs of our bodies, when healthy, attune to a particular set of harmonious vibrations. Should this harmony be disturbed and the body manifest illness or disease, colour – a form of vibrational healing – offers a powerful tool to help it return to a state of wholeness and balance.

Colour healing is defined as the use of visible and invisible light in order to bring harmony to the energetic fields of an individual.

Invisible light has long been employed in orthodox medical work; both **ultra-violet** (which has a higher frequency or vibrational level than violet) and **infra-red** (which has a lower frequency than red) will be familiar to you in this context.

Colour in history

Use of visible colours for healing purposes was widespread in Atlantis and Ancient Egypt. In *The Seven Keys to Colour Healing*, Roland Hunt describes temples designed for this purpose:

> *'In the ancient temples of Heliopolis, Egypt, the force of colour was used not only as an aid to worship, but as a healing agent. These temples were orientated so that the sun shone through in such a way its light was broken up into seven prismatic colours, and the suffering ones were bathed in that special colour they needed to restore them to health.'*

It is interesting to note that the colours used by artists in ancient cave-paintings differ from those used today, leading to speculation that thousands of years ago Man actually perceived a range of colours which was more limited than those we now recognise. In pre-historic art in Africa, Australia and Europe, primitive dark reds, oranges and ochre tones predominate. As colours associated with the lower chakras (see Chapter on The Chakras), they are symbolic of an environment and a way of life concerned almost exclusively with the physical world and with survival as seen in the hunter/gatherer. It is apparent that, at different stages of his evolution, Man has become increasingly sensitive to colours of higher frequencies.

Light theory

Visible light, which includes colour, is detected by light sensitive rods and cones in the human retina and is part of the electro-magnetic spectrum. There are, however, much higher frequencies of light present in the Universe, including Cosmic frequencies. These, which most of us cannot see with the naked eye, exist within the realm of what we perceive as darkness.

White light is said to symbolise Universal Intelligence with each of its constituent rainbow colours representing a specific aspect of that intelligence. Hence the significance attached by many mystics to the process of 'grounding the Light', or making manifest here on our planet the Universal qualities which light possesses.

Using a simple prism, pure, or 'white' light can be split into: magenta, violet, indigo, blue, green, yellow, orange and red.

Each of these has a **complementary colour**. These you can determine for yourself by means of a simple exercise.

Take a piece of coloured card or material. Hold it a comfortable distance from you. Focus your eyes and attention on it until the original colour begins to fade and is replaced by its complementary colour. Note your findings:

....

....

....

....

> ❀ An alternative method is to place the colour against a white background and focus for 1–2 minutes. Then take the colour away, and see what complementary colour appears against the white background. Note your findings:
>
> ....
> ....
> ....
> ....

You may like to compare your results with these recognised complementary pairings:

Magenta and green
Violet and yellow
Blue and orange
Turquoise and red

Colour and healing

Just as each colour has its own vibrational frequency, so do the organs of the human body and the subtle energetic bodies which constitute the spiritual human being. The combination of colours expressed by these various energies comprise the **aura** (see Chapter on The Chakras). The colours in the aura – which are visible to those with clairvoyance – will vary according to the individual's emotional state, their soul purpose, spiritual awareness, mental output and the health of their Physical Body.

Have you explored your own ability to see auras and the colours in them? If not, why not start now? The following hints may be helpful:

1 Auras are easier to see against a neutral or pale background.

2 They often appear like faint shadows surrounding people (or objects – everything in the plant or animal world possesses an aura, as do many apparently 'inanimate' objects like rocks and mountains).

3 Auras are sometimes easier to perceive if you allow your gaze to be unfocused – 'soften' your eyes.

4 At first, you may see auras as grey and without perceptible colour. You may later develop the ability to see colours quite clearly.

5 Be prepared to experiment with your 'inner vision' by working with your eyes shut. Some people 'see' the colours of the aura with their inner eyes.

It is no coincidence that when people are unwell, they are often described as being 'off-colour'. The foundation of colour healing is the understanding that when some part of a person's energetic structure is vibrating at a rate or frequency other than that which represents well-being, exposure to the appropriate light frequency can facilitate a return to health and harmony.

A rainbow for health

This exercise will enable you to experience for yourself the power of colour to regenerate and revitalise. Always pleasurable, it is particularly effective at times when you may feel run-down or when your 'batteries need recharging'.

The ideal preparation is to enter a space in which you feel relaxed and comfortable at all levels. Tuning in to each level in turn and 'breathing out' any concern, tension or distraction will aid the process.

❀   WHEN you are ready to begin, imagine yourself outdoors, in a place where you feel carefree and at ease. It may be a familiar place, perhaps a meadow, hillside or beach you have visited previously or it may be somewhere created by your imagination. Take time to connect with this environment; the colours, the feel of the ground underfoot, perhaps the smells and sounds.

❀   FIND a comfortable, relaxed position from which you can gaze into the sky. Allow the image to emerge of a brilliant rainbow, curving across the sky, its colours clear and vibrant. Take as long as you wish to savour this beautiful sight.

❀   ALLOW your attention to focus on the rainbow's red band. As you do so, imagine that band of colour gently separating from the others and moving slowly downward, towards you, in the form of sparkling light.

❀   AS it reaches you, allow that cloud of dancing, glistening red light to gently envelop your whole body. It touches you and becomes a mist so fine it passes through your skin.

❀   SLOWLY, as your body is suffused with red light, have a sense of receiving energy from the highest source of light you can imagine.

❀   WHEN both your body and aura have received as much of this vibration as they need right now, allow the excess to be released and absorbed into the air around you.

❀   REPEAT the process for each rainbow colour (red, orange, yellow, green, blue, indigo, violet) in turn,

taking all the time you need for your energy system to be fully replenished.

❀ WHEN you feel complete with the process, allow a new rainbow to form above you in the sky, ready for the next time you feel the need to avail yourself of its wonderful powers.

❀ FINALLY return your awareness gently, coming back to ordinary reality.

❀ You may find your system absorbs some colours more easily than others. Make a note below of those you found less easy to absorb; this often indicates an emotional or energetic block related to that colour. Regular use of this exercise helps to release such blockages.

....

....

....

The following list will help you recognise the issues which you may be addressing if you find yourself instinctively working with a particular colour:

Red: Security, sense of self

Orange: Relationships, sacredness

Yellow: Discernment, honesty and freshness

Green: Harmony, growth and compassion

Blue: Healing, calmness and authority

Indigo: Depth, clarity, focus and discrimination

Purple: Spirituality, nobility and connection

Silver: Wisdom and understanding

Gold: Creativity and divine compassion.

Colour awareness

Bearing in mind what you know about the significance of different colours, you will find it interesting and informative to observe the use of colours in everyday situations.

- Red restaurants mean fast food and quick service – don't look for a leisurely, romantic meal here!

- Blue is often used for authority figures such as policemen, traffic wardens and customs officers.

- Green is used by hospital staff to denote cleanliness and calmness. It also denotes freshness in vegetables, but would give the opposite message if used to package meat.

✿ What are your own associations with colours? In the space provided, jot down anything which comes to mind in connection with these colours.

Red ....
....

Orange ....
....

Yellow ....
....

Green ....
....

Blue ....
....

Indigo ....
....

Violet ....
....

Are there other colours which hold special significance for you?

....
....
....
....

Colour energies

Having experienced how it feels to absorb various colours into your body, it is now appropriate to examine in more detail what such an exercise can achieve. To do so, we look at:

- How to enhance certain personal qualities and characteristics by the use of particular colours.

- Which physical conditions and functions are most responsive to particular colours.

Colour	Qualities	Conditions which are alleviated
Red		
	Vitality	Low blood pressure
	Energy	Exhaustion
	Sexuality	Anaemia
	Will	Impotence
	Courage	Pneumonia
	Passion	

(Negative connotations: excess of red can exhaust you. Not recommended for diseases of the heart area. Negative qualities include violence, rage and intolerance.)

Orange		
	Happiness	Depression
	Creativity	Poor liver function
	Being outgoing and uplifting	Poor circulation
	Sacredness	Low calcium levels

Capacity to relate   Poor digestion

Playfulness

(Negative connotations include being overbearing, pessimistic and self-indulgent.)

Yellow

Brightness   Diabetes

Discernment   Rheumatism

Originality   Arthritis

Enthusiasm   Constipation

Mental stimulation

Optimism

(Negative connotations: yellow can be manipulative and critical, sarcastic, impatient and judgemental.)

Green

Connecting   Tension

Harmonising   Poor heart function

Balancing   Imbalanced cell growth

Stabilising

Inspirational

Generous

(Negative connotations: jealousy ('green with envy'), meanness, prejudice and suspiciousness.)

Turquoise

Alertness   Inflammation

Clarity   Cuts and burns

Speaking one's truth   Acne and skin problems

Self-sufficiency   Hay fever

Self-awareness   Colitis

(Negative connotations: can feel empty and separate; it can also signify over-tight emotional control and selfishness.)

Blue

Patience   Fever, high blood pressure

Authenticity   Anxiety

Devotion	Throat problems
Wisdom	Eye imbalances
Faith	Menstrual problems
Healing	Ear disease

(Negative connotations: association with doubts, tactlessness, emotional instability and intellectual deceit.)

Indigo

Focus	Visual imbalances
Self-responsibility	Sinus disease
Perception	Pain
Discrimination	
Intuition	
Fortitude	

(Negative connotations: can become overwhelmed and narrow-visioned, fanatical, self-righteous and addicted.)

Violet

Dignity	Glandular imbalances
Deep respect	Epilepsy
Spirituality	Concussion
Reverence	Bacterial and viral infections
Awareness of higher purpose	Neuralgia
Stillness	Worry

(Negative connotations: can be forgetful, can lead to depression, be impractical and too idealistic.)

Magenta

Dedication	Disorientation
Sensitivity to other dimensions	Inadequate circulation to brain
Commitment	Distrust
Compassion	Amnesia
Gratefulness	
Trust	

(Negative connotations: can become arrogant and snobbish, pompous and corrupt.)

Colour healing – applications

A number of the applications listed below (e.g. Solarized Water) do not require experts to put them into practice. They are ideal for you to experiment with yourself.

If you do try out some of the simpler methods, don't forget to keep a notebook handy so you can record the results.

Syntonics

This form of treatment was developed by Dr Harry Riley Spitler in the 1930s. He found by projecting different frequencies of the visible light spectrum through a patient's eyes, he could treat a range of bodily functions.

Aura-Soma

The individual chooses or is presented with bottles produced by Vicky Wall. They are filled with different coloured oils and water in accordance with their needs at that time. The particular combination of colours can be utilised by a trained practitioner to provide an holistic assessment and also as a treatment.

Solarized Water or coloured tinctures

This essentially simple process involves allowing sunlight to fall for at least two hours on a glass of water surrounded by a perspex filter of the required colour. The water is then sipped over the course of the day.

Coloured clothes or environments

A process which many of us may perform unconsciously is to use the colour of clothes or our surroundings to bring specific healing qualities. Coloured silk scarves, wrapped round certain parts of the body for 20 minutes or so, facilitate that particular colour entering the person's auric field.

 Try the following simple but effective exercise next time you experience pain in a particular part of the body e.g. headache, stomach ache, shoulder or neck pain.

- From your wardrobe, assemble items of different (preferably unmixed) colours. Small squares and scarves are ideal. (The wider the range of colours you have, the greater the scope for healing to take place.)

- Take a few moments to find a quiet space and go within.

- Using your Inner Healer, ask to be guided towards the colours which would have the most beneficial healing effect on the part of your body where you presently experience discomfort or disharmony.

- Take the item of the colour you have selected and wrap it gently round the affected part of the body.

- Leave it there for 10–15 minutes and make a note of any effects you experience.

Reflexology Torch/Acucolour Torch

Light from a special torch is projected through a crystal and coloured filter directly onto specific areas of the body in order to treat a variety of physical ailments, using the principles of reflexology or acupuncture.

Coloured oils

Coloured aromatherapy oils are used for massage, especially those using the natural colour of the essential oil – such as Lavender.

Rainbow diet

Those following this regime eat only fruit and vegetables of particular colours or groups of colours. Red, orange and yellow are colours for the morning, with blue and violet reserved for the evening and night. Green foods can be eaten at any time.

In addition to this simple diet, there are many other ways of consciously utilising food as a way of ingesting the colours we need to enhance and maintain our level of physical health. Fruit and vegetables – provided they are fresh – are also an excellent means of taking sunlight into the body.

Chromatherapy

This involves the use of different wavelengths and colour frequencies for healing purposes. Colours are projected directly onto the relevant part of the body, typically for periods between 10 and 20 minutes.

Hospital research has shown 'Blue Box' treatment – a simple form of coloured light therapy – to be highly effective in many cases of arthritis – especially those in which the hands are affected. Sufferers place their hands in a purpose-built, enclosed box for periods of 15–20 minutes, exposing them to light from a blue electric light bulb.

A number of patients, having discovered how effective regular treatment of this kind can be, have asked why the Blue Box is not available commercially. The answer seems to lie in the fact that it is so simple and so cheap to make, manufacturers see insufficient profit in producing and marketing it!

Colour therapy

This process involves the use of coloured slides to project light onto a human image. This is done in accordance with the specific needs of an individual who need not be physically present but who 'tunes in to' the healing process as it is being carried out.

Photodynamic therapy

This form of medical treatment involves the intravenous injection of certain light-sensitive chemicals which accumulate in the target cells. These chemicals show up under ultra-violet light, enabling the operator to detect the cells and intensify the ability of a fibro-optic laser to destroy them. This technique, which has proved highly successful and has low side effects, has been used in treating cancer, tumours, venereal warts and atherosclerosis.

Colour visualisation

Using the examples in this Chapter will give you first-hand experience of the power of this form of colour healing.

Practise playing with colour ...

If you find you are sensitive to colour and enjoy working with it, there are many ways to increase your awareness of it and the messages it carries.

What we wear

> ❋ **Notice and record the colours you choose to wear.** Can you relate them to your mood or emotional state as you make the selection?
>
> ....
> ....
> ....

> ❋ Are the colours you choose when you feel relaxed and happy any different from the ones you opt for when you feel tired or sad?
>
> ....
> ....
> ....
> ....

❀ You may find the colours demanded by your work may not match your mood. How does it feel when you experience such a 'mis-match'?

....
....
....
....

❀ When you see someone wearing particular colours, perhaps bright ones rather than subdued tones, you may find you make assumptions either about the person or the way they are feeling. If so, make a note of your response.

....
....
....
....

❀ When selecting clothes do you: Yes   No

1 Follow fashion?   ....
2 Dictate it?   ....
3 Buy and wear whatever meets your
   needs at that time?   ....
4 Buy what is an old favourite, year after
   year?   ....

Be adventurous; buy something to wear which expresses a part of yourself you usually keep hidden. Put it on – and see how that feels!

Nature

❋ Many of us have favourite flowers, or plants. Make a note of the colours which bring you special pleasure.

....
....
....
....

❋ How is your mood or emotional state affected by the various colours in nature?

....
....
....
....

Environment

❋ Look around your home or workplace. Is the decor in harmony with the needs of each space?

....
....
....
....

Yellow, for example, facilitates mental stimulation – ideal for an office or study, less so for a bedroom, since it makes it difficult for the mind to switch off.

✿ Are there rooms in your home (or other people's) in which you feel particularly comfortable (or uncomfortable)? Does the colour scheme in those rooms play a part in your response? If so, how?

....

....

....

....

✿ Did you choose the colours which surround you at home or were they there when you moved in (representing someone else's choices)? Do you find the colours and combinations of colour in each room harmonious and agreeable? If not, how important is it to you to change them? Do you plan to change them, and if so, how soon?

....

....

....

....

Star colour healing

In the exercise which follows, allow your intuition to select and utilise the colour your energy system particularly needs right now. It may also inspire you to use your creativity to develop your own unique set of colour healing exercises.

This very simple process is particularly valuable when there is limited time available. Try it when you are away from home and unable to create the ideal environment, yet you feel the need to be calmer, more 'centred' or better equipped to deal with the demands on your energy system.

With practice you may be able to perform this exercise in a crowded place such as a train, simply closing your eyes and going to your quiet space within. If that is not yet possible, do your best to find somewhere you can be alone and quiet.

❁ MAKING yourself comfortable, close your eyes, and begin by taking a few deep breaths. Each time you exhale, have a sense of gently expelling any stress or tension in your system.

❁ WHEN you feel ready, imagine yourself lying on the ground in a place you feel at ease, secure and safe, gazing up into a clear night sky. Far above you, imagine the stars are shining forth many colours. Allow yourself a few moments to simply enjoy the beauty of this vision.

❁ AS you gaze at the stars, become aware that one of them has a special gift for you; one of them holds the special qualities which will fulfil your energetic needs right now. Let go of any idea of choosing a favourite colour, and allow your inner knowing to tell you which of those many stars it may be.

❁ ONCE 'your' star has made itself known, allow it to send towards you a powerful, pulsating ray of its coloured light. Bathe in the glow of that 'celestial spotlight'; see how the colour feels on your body.

❋   WHEN you are ready, breathe in the light, drawing it into every part of your body. Allow it to permeate both your physical and energetic structure, trusting it to give you whatever qualities you need to meet the challenges of the moment.

❋   WHEN you feel you have drawn in all the colour energy you need, release any excess, and allow the ray of colour to return to your chosen star.

❋   SLOWLY return your awareness to the room, or the place of 'ordinary reality', wrapped in the essence of your particular colour.

Working with colour is a delightful way of connecting with revitalising, nurturing and healing vibrations. In addition to the colours mentioned here, many people enjoy using sparkling golden and silver light in visualisations and other meditational exercises. Golden light brings the highest form of compassion, and silver brings wisdom.

Use your imagination and creativity to create your unique experiences with colour, and be sure to record them in your journal.

Sharing your experiences of colour allows other people to enjoy and partake in one of the natural gifts of our Universe.

Sound

'... Wherever men have trodden they have left a trail of song; and ... these trails must reach back, in time and space, to an isolated pocket in the African Savannah, where the First Man shouted the opening stanza of the World Song, "I am!"'

THE SONG LINES – BRUCE CHATWIN

The healing potential of sound, in common with that of colour, is slowly gaining acceptance amongst medical practitioners here in the West. However, the use of sound has always been associated with shamanic work, the most ancient expression of healing known to man and one with traditions stretching back thousands of years.

The use of drums and rattles is widespread in shamanic practice, and the rattles still given to babies are an acknowledgement of the healing power of this instrument. A story related to me by a friend is a reminder of just how powerful traditional rattles are:

'The mother of a three week old baby had come to stay with us. The baby cried a great deal, sometimes for extended periods, which his mother found distressing. One evening, with the baby crying inconsolably, I responded to an intuitive impulse by fetching a rattle I had made – from natural materials – on a shamanic healing course. Gently, I began to rattle the baby's aura. Within two or three minutes the crying had stopped. He lay peacefully in his amazed mother's arms, soon drifting off to sleep.'

Throughout history, rhythm, sound and song have been employed in the healing arts. This reflects the understanding that we ourselves, for all our appearance of solidity are, in truth, pure vibration.

Historical records inform us that in the ancient kingdoms of Assyria, Sumeria and Babylonia, musicians were also priests who carried out astrological calculations as part of their healing work. In the temples of ancient Greece, Egypt and Rome, we know priests chanted incantations as they administered medicine to the sick.

In those days, healer-priests were familiar with sacred geometry and its application in producing harmonics, musical intervals and rhythms which constituted the world soul. Using this knowledge, music has been employed to reach the inner essence of the individual and hence help them harmonise with their own inner note.

Pythagoras, the Greek philosopher, proposed a theory of the 'music of the spheres'. According to this, as the planets moved through space each one created a different sound all of which were harmonically linked. His interest in music went further, for he also used it as an instrument of healing.

The school Pythagoras established taught wisdom on three levels. In the first, instruction was given regarding musical proportions and harmonics. In the second, pupils learned the mathematics of music and also self-control. At the highest level, pupils were acquainted with the mysteries of vibrational healing through the medium of sound and music.

Sound in your life

We are constantly surrounded by sound – some of it harmonious and pleasing, some disturbing on a subtle level. Noise pollution is a greater hazard than physical pollution, since it is more insidious and individual.

> ❀ **Take time to think about your experience of sound.**
> List below sounds, natural or man-made, which evoke these
> responses from you:
>
> Joy ....
> Fear ....
> Sadness ....
> Anticipation ....
> Calmness ....
> Excitement ....
> Inspiration ....
> Anger ....

Our sound comes from the heart. However, many people have
experienced having their singing criticised or even ridiculed by
insensitive teachers or parents. In some cases, this results in the 'still
voice' of the heart being shut down.

On the other hand, in some educational systems, the importance
of sound and music is fully acknowledged. In Rudolph Steiner schools,
for example, a musical element is incorporated into every lesson,
whatever the subject may be.

Silence is golden

It is common for people to fear silence because they believe that
without music or voice they cannot function within the world. Silence
also allows into consciousness powerful inner thoughts. These may
be uncomfortable and are therefore customarily blocked out by
constant stimulus – including sound – from the outer world. This may
partly explain the omnipresent pop music in our society – especially
in places frequented by young people.

Everybody has experience of creating sound. This may be anything
from singing in the shower to expert musicianship.

Write down what sounds you make and how you feel when you make them.

....
....
....
....
....
....

Sound theory

Light and sound occur on a different range of vibrational frequencies, or wavelengths, as illustrated below:

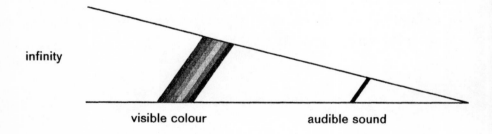

infinity

visible colour   audible sound

When the frequency of electro-magnetic energy is slowed down further beyond the range of colour, the narrow band of audible sound vibration is reached. The cochlea of the ear is sensitive to frequencies between 16 and 16,000 hertz, although many older people cannot hear those higher than 10,000 hertz.

Examples of the power of sound include the Biblical story of the walls of Jericho, the ability of singers to shatter glass with their voices alone, and the necessity for soldiers to break step when crossing bridges, in case the vibrational harmonic created by rhythmic pacing causes the structure to collapse.

Cymatics – sound creating structure

In the eighteenth century, a German violinist named Chladni placed sand on a thin metal plate, and drew his bow across it. He discovered that the application of a single tone in this way caused the sand to form itself into interlocking and concentric circles. Chladni called this effect of sound waves on matter *cymatics*, and in the early twentieth century his work was further developed by Swiss scientist Hans Jenny.

Jenny experimented with many different substances, including sand, dust and even water, applying single-tone sounds including classical music as well as the human voice both speaking and singing. He discovered that materials behave in a predictable rather than a random manner, and that the process mirrors the growth patterns of living organisms such as cells, bones, chromosomes and even crystals.

When certain Hebrew and Sanskrit words were spoken, some material actually took on the shape of the words themselves, although the same was not true of modern languages. Jenny concluded that:

> *'Throughout the animal and vegetable kingdoms, Nature creates in rhythms, periods, frequencies, reduplications, serial phenomenon, sequence etc. How Nature proceeds in these matters is the question.'*

He believed the key to healing the body with specific tones lay in understanding how frequency acts upon genes, cells and other structures of the body. Only then, he thought, would we understand the exact frequency of the body itself.

A body/sound experience

You will need equipment for playing the piece of music you select. A Walkman offers good quality sound especially as the earphones minimise distraction from external sound sources. Have pen and notebook to hand to make a record of your experience.

❀   Select a piece of music which you find calming, soothing and relaxing.

❀   Take time to find a quiet place to go within, using breathing to let go of any pressures or tensions of which you are aware.

❀   Closing your eyes, listen to the music you chose. As you do so, gently scan your body.

Where in your body do you 'feel' the music?

....
....
....
....
....

Does it evoke sensations or images? What effect does the music have on that part of your body?

....
....
....
....
....

❀   Enjoy the experience!

The healer/therapist as an instrument of entrainment

Entrainment is a phenomenon of sound in which a powerful rhythmic vibration emanating from one object excites a similar but less power-ful vibration from another. The second object locks in step, oscillating at the first object's rate. This is the mechanism by which energy is preserved in Nature.

Much vibrational healing – not music therapy alone – uses this principle in order to recreate harmony. In such cases, the therapist supplies the more powerful vibration, which exerts a strong influence on the weaker vibration of the patient.

Studies on vibrational healing are rarely significant in statistical research terms, because, through entrainment, they are open to influence by the attitudes of both those being researched and those carrying out the studies.

This principle highlights the importance of **intent** and **frequency**. The intention or focus within the mind, acts as the controlling force in the dynamic. It entrains other sub-atomic elements to realign to a specific frequency, hence *intent* at this level is more powerful than genius for, as Jonathan Goldman says:

INTENT + FREQUENCY = HEALING

What you *think* influences your reality more than what you *do*; it is important that the two should be in harmony.

At some level – almost certainly an unconscious one – in the therapeutic setting, the therapist's intent will create an harmonic within the client. Therapists should therefore ensure they act with the intent of goodness and compassion; first applying these values to themselves.

Sound signature – Sharry Edwards

Sharry Edwards' gift is the ability to listen to someone's speech and identify which notes are missing from it. She is then able to interpret these 'sound gaps' in terms of the emotional trauma from which they result. Her work demonstrates that a gap disappears when the trauma to which it relates is resolved. Sharry is also gifted with heightened hearing, extending well outside the normal human range, and she can pick up and relay another person's 'signature sound'.

Practitioners including Sharry Edwards and Dr Alfred Tomatis base their therapeutic work on the understanding that whenever we experience stress which is not expressed, it results in the loss of certain notes of the octaves related to speech. (Note how we unconsciously modify our voice when we speak to someone who is grieving, tending towards monotony or single tone.)

With the aid of specially developed instruments it is now possible to detect these absent tones and provide the client with a recording of them. Re-experiencing them can help the individual to get in touch once more with the suppressed emotion, and thus facilitate a return to balance. A similar system is used to aid physical symptoms, under-lining the link between sound and matter.

The healing song

Many ancient cultures acknowledge that every human being has a unique healing song, as well as an inner soul melody or note. Finding this note is often seen as the exclusive gift of the shaman but all of us have that ability. Watch children as they spontaneously hum or sing songs of happiness while they play. Also listen to the sounds they utter when they are in pain.

 Are you aware of songs or melodies you habitually sing, whistle or hum in particular situations?

....

....

....

....

....

At a certain age, we become more self-conscious, and the voice or song disappears within. In many cases we are prevented from singing by fear of being judged. In oriental medicine the tongue is linked to the heart; when the tongue is quiet the heart dies. Release of sound is highly therapeutic, and when sound is created through right intent, it has the power to reach deep within the soul.

❀

Music and mood

Music can be a great mood-modifier; many people will testify that singing or whistling a happy song can change a dark mood to a light one with amazing rapidity. It can also evoke memories, and instinctively we may tend to avoid music which reminds us of painful experiences.

A participant on one of my *Spirit in Practice* courses described how, as an eight year old, he had been sent to boarding school – a painful experience for him. The wife of the headmaster was an accomplished pianist and he used to lie in bed at night listening to her playing Beethoven. It was many years, he told me, before he could listen to classical music without feeling once again the sadness and loneliness he had experienced at that time.

The skill of music therapists lies in aiding the release of stored emotions, in the process giving the individual the opportunity to move into a state of improved emotional, mental and physical health.

❈   In this exercise you are invited to imagine you have been asked to take part in 'Desert Island Discs'. Have pen and notebook to hand to make a record of your experience.

❈   Choose four pieces of music which are available to you at this time, and which have strong associations with particular periods or events in your life. When selecting these periods or events, choose some with positive connotations, and some with negative connotations.

❈   Before beginning, be aware of your mood – how you feel at this moment. Make a note of it in your book.

❈   Make yourself comfortable, then settle down to listen to the first piece of music. Allow it to connect you to the relevant period or experience.

❈   As you listen to the music, be aware of what images or memories it evokes.

❈   When the music is over, note any alterations in your mood caused by listening to that piece of music and the experiences with which you associate it.

❈   Repeat the exercise with the other pieces of music, allowing sufficient time between them for you to 'clear' yourself of the preceding experience.

Shamanic practice, drumming and music therapy

In music therapy, the role of the therapist is similar to that of the shaman, who was present at all rites of passage, healings and major ceremonies. The shaman traditionally employs music, drumming, rattling or chanting in order to minimise distraction from their left brain.This is done whilst entraining electrical impulses from the more subconscious part of the brain in order to entrain other brain states. Shaman and patient together then travel to a place of altered consciousness, where the Inner Healer resides and true healing can occur.

Michael Harner, an authority on shamanic traditions, suggests that such sounds 'may have the latent function of affecting the central nervous system activity in a manner analogous to yogic breathing exercises'. On the role of the human voice he offers that:

'The change into a shamanic state of consciousness is also helped by singing. The shaman typically has special 'power songs' that he chants on such occasions. While the words may vary somewhat from shaman to shaman in a particular tribe, usually the melody and rhythm of the songs are not the invention of the individual shaman but are shared in a particular tribal region.'

Michael Harner – *The Way of the Shaman*

There is general agreement in regard to drumming that:

- It is a rhythmic stimulus in trance inducement.

- It sedates the shaman's left brain activity through distraction, allowing the right hemisphere to journey to the spirit world.

- It promotes alpha brain waves.

- It sends the patient into a trance-like state, thus enhancing their belief in the shaman.

- It aids the therapist to achieve similar response in modern medicine without the therapist necessarily entering the same state.

Dr Alfred Tomatis, a French authority on auditory neurophysiology, states that drumming, being of low frequency, should always be accompanied by sound of a higher frequency. This is necessary to prevent over-stimulation of fluid within the inner ear. He also feels that low frequencies fail to adequately stimulate the brain, possibly resulting in exhaustion.

The combination of music and imagery is widely used in healing work, and is proven to work particularly effectively in:

- the alleviation of pain
- aiding disease control (notably in cases of diabetes)
- reducing anxiety, stress and depression
- enhancing immunity (notably in cases of cancer and AIDS).

Also used in music therapy are Sound Creation Gongs. Untuned and 11 in number, they are from the Indonesian tradition. They produce relatively unknown, spontaneous sounds which frequently elicit emotional releases.

There are many other ways in which sound, including music and song, can evoke suppressed emotions. This route to accessing stored emotion is important, since if it remains unexpressed it frequently results in physical illness.

Chanting

Chanting is an ancient method of healing using the human voice. It employs the principle of harmonics, which are the product of a single tone and its overtones. Life is a series of ever-changing harmonics, influenced by the interplay of energies within our environment, and the medium through which we are receiving our energy.

Overtones can be produced by using the voice or any instrument, notably Tibetan Bowls. The Tibetans and Mongolians are renowned for their chants, in which they produce overtones by modifying their breathing, nasal passages and tongue positions.

Among the most famous examples of harmonic chanting are the sixth century Gregorian chant, and Indian Khyal singing. The former is unique, as there is no meter; timing is based on breath rather than written rhythm. The chant covers the whole range of human hearing, stimulating all parts of the brain and increasing well-being by a relatively rapid rise through the scale. In the opinion of Dr Tomatis: '*... the sounds of Gregorian are a uniquely fantastic energy food ... it is the beat of a calm heart, the rhythm of a tranquil heart.*'

Chanting through the chakras

Chanting has been shown to be a highly effective method of 'tuning' the chakras. Research carried out on the effects of sacred chanting indicates high-frequency chants actually stimulate the central nervous system. This was borne out by the experience of a community of Tibetan monks when they were forbidden to include the customary chanting in their devotions. Within a very short period they were struck by several forms of physical illness, notably sickness, depression, tiredness and insomnia.

The table below indicates the sounds which have been found to relate most closely to the vibration of the chakras and the physical conditions relating to them which are most likely to benefit from the appropriate chants:

Chakra	Application	Note
Crown	Depression Parkinson's disease	EE (see) *(said with mouth almost closed)*
Third Eye	Visual problems Sinusitis Tension headaches Migraines	AY (say) *(said with mouth almost closed)*
Throat	Breathing problems Neck pains Throat problems Under active thyroid Hearing loss	I (eye)
Heart	Heart imbalances Cancer AIDS Allergies Auto immune problems	AH
Solar Plexus	Digestive disorders Liver disease Duodenal ulcers Diabetes Gallstones	OH!

Sacral	Constipation	OO (cool)
	Menstrual disorders	
	Irritable bowel	
	Infertility	
Base	Hypertension	UH
	Piles	
	Arthritis	
	Anxiety	
	Epilepsy	
	Kidney disorders	

Discovering your healing tones

Allow yourself 15–20 minutes for this exercise. You will require a space in which you are comfortable to experiment with your voice. If you have concerns about being overheard, perhaps you can find a secluded place outdoors or in the shower where you will also be able to experience Nature's healing energies! Don't forget your notebook and pen or pencil.

You will need to take with you a copy of the above table, giving you the notes corresponding to each chakra.

❀ STANDING, sitting or lying in a comfortable, relaxed position, close your eyes and take three or four deep breaths, releasing any stress or tension in your body as you exhale.

❋ TAKE your awareness first to your Base chakra.

❋ ONCE you feel attuned to that chakra, begin to chant the note UH. Experiment by moving from the Base chakra up and then down until you discover the tone which feels most in harmony with your Base chakra. When you have the right note, repeat it three times.

❋ CONTINUE to chant until the chakra feels fully nurtured by the sound. Then let go of that chakra and move on to the Sacral. Repeat the process, this time using the note OO (as in cool).

❋ ONCE you reach the EE, give yourself time to stay at the Crown's sound, and feel the energy around you. Then, when you are ready, repeat three OO's to bring you back down, and to allow a gentle return to reality.

DURING THIS EXERCISE, YOU MAY EXPERIENCE CHANGES IN THE STATE OF YOUR CHAKRAS, AND IMAGES OR COLOURS MAY PRESENT THEMSELVES. IF SO, RECORD THEM IN YOUR NOTEBOOK.

The healing potential of sound – notably in the form of song – is enjoying a widespread renaissance, bearing out the view of Jonathan Goldman, sound-therapist and author, that 'disease is simply part of our body vibrating out of tune'. There are many workshops available for those drawn to working with their voice, and also those who enjoy combining movement – in the form of dance – with music.

The Intuitive Practitioner

'It is the heart always that sees, before the head can see.'
Thomas Carlyle, Chartism 1839

We live in an age which places a high premium on the ability to use rational processes, notably logic, to provide us with answers to everyday problems. As a result many people – particularly men – may scarcely be aware of the extent to which they rely on their intuition.

As you answer these questions, you may gain insight into how often you use your intuition:

> When faced with a range of choices, how do you decide:
>
> Where you are going to sit on a bus or train?
> Who you are going to talk to at a party?
> Which house you are going to buy?
> Which school you will choose for your child?
> When you will leave to get to an appointment?
> What colour or style of clothes you are going to wear today?

❀ **Using the space below, list other situations in which you feel guided by intuition.**

....

....

....

....

....

....

....

What is intuition?

The exercise of intuition represents an important step forward in mankind's development, replacing exaggerated reliance on purely intellectual processes by greater balance between head and heart. As a function of the mind, it can be defined as *the synthesis of intellect and emotion through the appropriate use of its constituent parts.*

Before we are fully able to utilise this source of inner guidance, we must achieve a new relationship with certain other functions of the mind. People have become reliant on logic, emotions and instincts in order to get their needs met – and in doing so become slaves to these functions. The new relationship involves moving into a position of mastery.

In practical terms, by becoming **master** instead of **slave**, we use our:
Instinct – for creativity rather than simply for survival
Emotion – in order to connect with rather than separate from
Logic – in order to focus, not to limit.

From the esoteric perspective, intuition is closely linked to our Third Eye which relates to *our intention to create,* and our Heart chakra, which relates to *compassion and resonance with our truth.* (See also the Chapter on The Chakras.)

When intuition is active, we compare all advice, ideas and thoughts with the inner note of our heart. If they resonate, we respond by allowing them to penetrate more deeply into our consciousness. If not, we let them go.

The Third Eye provides focus and motivation from a place of objectivity and discernment, following the inspiration through the Crown chakra.

Acting on intuition

Arising from deep within our being, intuition guides us without coercion, threats, or promise of reward.

Following the **Universal Law of Attraction**, if we act on the intuitive impulse, energised by the power of love, we attract towards us only that which, on a soul level, brings the greatest benefit to all concerned – including, of course, ourselves.

As a level of consciousness which can accept our fears and limiting beliefs and move beyond them, intuition provides us with clarity of thought and the ability to make decisions without fear or regret.

Since it is not an intellectual process, it is important not to try to make sense of an intuitive impulse – just act on it! Don't worry if the objective is not initially evident. Following your intuition is the path to soul fulfilment – despite the fact that the ultimate goal or purpose may be hidden at the start of the journey.

... *or not!*

> ❀ Listed below are some of the most common reasons for not following through on intuitive hunches. Tick the ones you recognise in your life.
>
> Many of them relate to fear – one of the most potent inhibitors to intuition.
>
> Fear of failure: 'If I fail, I would feel humiliated.'   ......
> Fear of success: 'Other people would then expect
> too much of me.'   ......
> Lack of trust: 'What if it is my ego talking, or just my
> imagination?'   ......
> Believing the message is illogical: 'And logic rules in
> our world.'   ......
> Last time it led me astray: 'And I'm not doing that again.'......
> It doesn't fit with my game-plan: 'So it can't be right.'   ......
> Others would suffer: 'And they would blame me.'   ......
> It would mean I'd have to change: 'And anything is
> better than that!'   ......
>
> ❀ This space is for you to add any inhibitors of your own.
>
> ....
> ....
> ....
> ....
> ....

Logic is important for focusing our intuitive ideas, but should not be allowed to limit us – something which often results if we insist on applying logic to situations. Intuition is related to right brain activity, while linear thinking and logic, the realm of the left hemisphere of the brain, block the flow and build attachment. This is also likely to occur when we place too much reliance on belief systems or dogmas. They may provide structure to our life, but can also 'box us in'.

It is important not to confuse intuition with 'gut feeling' for the two are quite different. Gut feelings emanate from the Solar Plexus, their purpose being to help us achieve self-worth and self-value. Acting alone, the solar plexus operates to maintain our personal power, *at the expense of others if necessary.* In this it is quite different from intuition which, as we have seen, brings benefit to all *at the expense of none.*

Gut feelings are purely sensations, similar to smell, taste and touch. Although most of us continually pick up scents and sounds, we have a filter system which means we react only to those which benefit us at that time. Likewise, it is important to learn discrimination to prevent us reacting automatically to every gut feeling we experience.

At this time in mankind's history, the solar plexus is working overtime, often creating excessive reactions to situations which are not life-threatening. On a physical level, this heightened sensitivity may well be responsible for an increased level of allergies.

Specific physical sensations often accompany messages from the intuition. These include:

- tingling aura (see Chapter on The Chakras)
- tingling on the surface of skin (goose bumps, hairs standing up)
- shivers up the spine
- warmth round the heart
- pressure at the back of the head.

Equally, when intuitive impulses are ignored, there may be overwhelming physical symptoms, which may be taken as warnings to change direction – and soon!

Intuition and illness

Some people listen to their intuition only when forced to do so by illness. This is a time when their logical, practical mind is less active, and there is more opportunity for them to focus – consciously or unconsciously – on the needs of the soul.

The body is one of the most powerful communication points for our intuition; when the body is in distress, we are often left with no option but to listen. In such a situation, intuition expresses itself in a variety of ways:

> ❋ **Through the particular site of the illness.**
> Ask yourself what is your intuitive response to dis-ease in this organ or system? What is its function? Could dis-ease in this area have anything to do with your life in general?
> e.g. Do you feel blocked? (Constipation.)
> Do you feel unsupported or frightened to move? (Lower back pain.)
> Are you overwhelmed by a particular situation? (Indigestion.)
>
> ❋ **Through the words you use to describe the illness.**
> e.g. I feel 'tied up in knots'. (Irritable bowel disease.)
> There's a lump in my throat. (Does something need to be expressed?)
> I feel like I'm carrying the world on my shoulders. (Are you?)
>
> ❋ **Through acknowledging the effects of the illness.**
> e.g. What does it prevent you from achieving? (This may be positive or negative.)
> What would you do if you were well?
> What opportunities have presented themselves since you were ill?

For practitioners, one of the great benefits of employing intuition is that it provides them with increased diagnostic skills, involving more than the physical body alone. It also helps them to decide on the most appropriate treatment with confidence.

Illness may be the only way the soul can attract your attention.

The benefits of using intuition

The true energy of intuition is to take what is inwardly sensed and apply wisdom and compassion, knowing when to speak and when to stay silent. Often the message prompts us to regain our inner power – which may mean *standing clear of the tribe*. In this context, 'tribe' includes any group which exerts a powerful influence on the way we think or act. Examples include: partnership, family, religious affiliation, sports or social group, work or business organisation.

Developing intuition is an art. For most of us it was a gift acquired early in life, but one in which we lost faith because others (i.e. adults) failed to affirm it, or may even have actively devalued it through messages like: 'use your head'.

Failure to listen to intuition is often compounded by giving our power away to those we perceive as being 'in authority' i.e. knowing better than we do. As children, yielding our power to parents and teachers is virtually unavoidable. For some adults this pattern continues, with religious leaders and politicians favoured recipients.

Intuition is often a 'wake-up call' asking us to step into our personal power instead of relinquishing it to others. If we listen to the call, and act on it, it has the power to enhance the quality of our life in a number of important ways:

- Teaching us the art of looking beyond the obvious.
- Recognising the strength and beauty of waiting for the right moment to act.
- Encouraging us to act with detached compassion, seeing beyond the initial reaction.
- Guiding us through eddies of illusion.
- Helping us to avoid game-playing (which can be very addictive).
- Teaching us how to handle energy without the need to abuse the power.
- Helping us let go of belief systems which no longer serve us.
- Providing us with clarity of thought, and the ability to make decisions without fear or regret.

When intuition gives us access to inner strength, resulting in a merging of ego with soul, we reach a point at which we no longer perceive ourselves as separate from the Source.

Intuition then becomes a state of being rather than a means of doing.

A meditation to enhance the intuition

Linking the heart centre to the crown centre
You will recall that the intuitive process involves inspiration passing from the Crown chakra to the Heart chakra. Carrying out this exercise will help strengthen the link between the two.

Begin by finding yourself a comfortable, relaxed position, sitting or lying down. Take off your shoes, and loosen any tight clothing. Make sure you will be free from interruption, distraction or disturbance; this will help you gain the maximum from the experience.

Take a few deep breaths, in through the nose and out through the mouth, letting go of any tension in the body as you exhale.

✸ MOVING your attention to your Heart chakra, imagine entering the heart itself. There is a window in the heart, through which a glorious golden light is flooding. The source of the light is not apparent, but you feel inspired to find it.

✸ FINDING a door in the heart, you open it and step through. You find yourself in a corridor, along which the light is shining.

✸ WALK up the corridor, drawn forward by the light, until you realise you are standing totally in the light. Feel the marvellous, energising rays enter every part of your being, every cell of your body, refreshing, renewing and healing, until you are aware you and the light are one.

✸ TAKE time to experience and enjoy that sense of unity with the light.

✸ WHEN you are ready, retrace your steps, back along the corridor, but this time draw the light back down the corridor with you. Breathe in the light noticing it does not slip back to its original position.

❀ STEP back into your heart, allowing it to fill with this beautiful, powerful energy, knowing that on each beat of your heart, this light with its inspiration will spread through every cell in your body.

THROUGH THIS EXERCISE YOU ARE ENHANCING THE STRONG LINK BETWEEN HEART AND CROWN CHAKRAS, BETWEEN THE HEAD AND THE HEART, BETWEEN THE ETERNAL FLAME AND THE ETERNAL BREATH.

REPETITION OF THIS EXERCISE UNTIL YOU CAN EASILY IMAGINE A PATH OF LIGHT BETWEEN THE HEART AND THE TOP OF THE HEAD WILL HELP ENSURE ENHANCED INTUITIVE CONSCIOUSNESS.

Routes to enhancing your intuition

Meditation

Meditation is a way to still the logical mind and bring it under the guidance of Higher Consciousness. Let go of any expectations regarding the outcome – they block the flow of your Higher Wisdom.

Dreams

Dreams are a means whereby the soul communicates with the Lower Self. In Ancient Greece, dreams were sometimes performed by actors with the dreamer amongst the audience. In this way they could become objective observers of their subconscious, imitating the role of the intuition. This gave them the opportunity to understand the dream in relation to their soul's purpose.

The arts

The records of civilisations down the ages confirm that painting, sculpture, dance, drama, poetry, story-telling and song have always been seen as methods of accessing the deepest reaches of the mind.

The media

How often have you opened a newspaper or switched on the TV or radio to find yourself reading, watching or listening to something which is *exactly* what you needed at that moment? Of course, much of the information will simply drift past our conscious state, but be aware of those '*Ah-ha, yes!*' experiences!

Other people

Anyone – friend, family, or complete stranger – may say or do something which reflects your own Inner Knowing. And you, of course, do this for other people. How often has someone said to you: 'You know, something you said to me has been so useful ... ' (And very often you don't even remember saying it!)

Nature

Developing the ability to interpret messages from our natural environment helps develop our intuitive powers. Australian Aborigines, American Indians, Eskimos and other indigenous races rely heavily on the natural world to relay information from the spirit world.

The exercise which follows will help you develop your attunement to nature and in doing so help you enhance the power of your intuition.

Allow plenty of time for this exercise: at least an hour is ideal. Take a notebook and pencil with you so you can make a record of your experience.

❁ TAKE yourself to a place in Nature where you feel comfortable and at ease.

❁ SEEK permission from Mother Earth to work in this special place. Stand until your senses have become accustomed to the sounds, scents and textures of that place.

❁ ASK within that you should be drawn towards a tree, rock or place on the ground which is in harmony with your own soul essence.

> YOU MAY FIND YOUR SPECIAL PLACE EASILY, OR YOU MAY WISH TO USE YOUR BODY AS A DIVINING ROD. TO DO THIS, WALK ROUND THE AREA, PREFERABLY CLOCKWISE, USING YOUR LEFT HAND (PALM DOWN) AS A RECEIVER OF ENERGY. AS YOU APPROACH YOUR SACRED SPACE, YOUR HAND MAY TINGLE OR BECOME WARM.

❁ WHEN you sense you have found your particular place, stop. Make yourself comfortable so you can experience a special form of connection.

❁ HERE, in your sacred space, you may find stillness, strength, wisdom, unity, the answer to a question, or you may simply be open to whatever arises.

❈ WHEN complete with the experience, thank the tree, rock or special place, and leave quietly.

MAKE A NOTE OF ANY THOUGHTS OR IMAGES WHICH COME TO MIND.

The intuitive response

Learning to 'go with the flow' is the key to intuitive success. Recognising that the initial direction and goal can be changed at any time, be prepared to be flexible and alert to such changes.

Some people fear that by listening to the 'still, small voice' they might be in some way relinquishing control of their life. In fact, the reverse is true; the voice is their own inner knowing, and whether they follow its guidance or not is always a matter of choice, and free will.

Choose to trust and act on inner urges with strength of purpose, letting go of attachment to the outcome of your actions, whilst taking full responsibility for your decisions.

Intuition always works with the greater picture, overshadowing the needs and desires of the personal ego.

Questions associated with the intuitive response include:

- What do I need to reach my greatest potential?
- What can I learn from this experience?
- What do I need to change to feel better in this situation?
- What can I do to help clear the air?
- How can I help others know what I'm feeling?

We hope you have enjoyed this work book and that it will be a constant companion for a healthy mind, body and spirit.

For those wishing to learn about intuition and the intuitive process in depth, my book *Beyond the Obvious* (C W Daniel Company Ltd) will be of special interest.

Reading List

For those interested in learning more about the previously mentioned forms of therapy, the following books are recommended:

Stress

Leon Chaitlow	*Your Complete Stress-Proofing Programme*	Thorsons 1983
Kenneth R Pelletier	*Mind as Healer; Mind as Slayer*	Allen & Unwin 1978

Psychoneuroimmunology (PNI)

Deepak Chopra	*Quantum Healing*	Bantam 1989
	Unconditional Life	Bantam 1991
Bernie Siegel	*Peace, Love and Healing*	Perennial Library 1990
	Love, Medicine and Miracles	Harper & Row 1986
Joan & Miroslav Borysenko	*The Power of the Mind to Heal*	Eden Grove 1994
Lawrence Le Shan	*You Can Fight for Your Life*	Thorsons 1984
Sogyal Rinpoche	*The Tibetan Book of Living and Dying*	Rider Books 1992
Susan Jeffers	*Feel the Fear and Do it Anyway*	Arrow Books 1987
Dr Alan Watkins	*Mind-Body Medicine*	Churchill-Livingstone 1997

Henry Dreher	*The Immune Power*	
	Personality	Plume/Penguin 1995
Candace Pert	*Molecules of Emotion*	Simon & Schuster 1997

The Opportunity of Illness

Larry Dossey	*Healing Words*	HarperCollins 1993
Thorwald Dethlefsen	*The Healing Power of Illness*	
& Rudiger Hahlk		Element 1983
Louise Hay	*You Can Heal Your Life*	Eden Grove 1984
Christine Page	*Frontiers of Health*	C W Daniel 1992
	The Mirror of Existence	C W Daniel 1995
Arnold Mindell	*The Shaman's Body*	HarperCollins 1993
Hal Stone &		
Sidra Winkelman	*Embracing Ourselves*	Nataraj 1989
Stephen Levine	*Healing Into Life and Death*	Gateway 1989
Dr Christiane	*Women's Bodies, Women's*	
Northrup	*Wisdom*	Piatkus 1995
Marc Ian Barasch	*The Healing Path*	Penguin/Arkana 1995
Adriana Rocha &		
Kristi Jorde	*Child of Eternity*	Piatkus 1996

Chakras

Christine Page	*Frontiers of Health*	C W Daniel 1992
Caroline Myss	*Anatomy of the Spirit*	Bantam 1996
Caroline Myss	*Why People Don't Heal and*	
	How They Can	Bantam 1998
David Tansley	*The Raiment of Light*	Arkana 1983
	Ray Paths and Chakra	
	Gateways	C W Daniel 1985
	Chakras – Rays and	
	Radionics	C W Daniel 1988
	Radionics and the Subtle	
	Anatomy of Man	C W Daniel 1985
Alice Bailey	*Esoteric Healing*	Lucis Publishing 1984
Dr Richard Gerber	*Vibrational Healing*	Bear & Co 1988

The Intuitive Practitioner

Christine Page	*Beyond The Obvious*	C W Daniel 1998
	The Mirror of Existence	C W Daniel 1995
Alice Bailey	*Esoteric Healing*	The Lucis Trust 1953
	A Treatise on White Magic	The Lucis Trust 1951
Nancy Rosanoff	*The Intuition Workbook*	Aslan Publishing 1988
Belleruth Naparstek	*Your Sixth Sense*	HarperCollins 1997

Colour Healing

Jacob Liberman	*Light, Medicine of the Future*	Bear & Co 1991
Theophilus Gimbel	*The Colour Therapy Workbook*	Element 1993
Betty Wood	*The Healing Power of Colour*	Aquarian Press 1989
Lilian Verner Bonds	*Discover the Magic of Colour*	Optima 1993
Lilla Bek & Annie Wilson	*What Colour Are You?*	Aquarian 1981

Sound

Don Campbell	*Music Physician*	Quest Books 1992
Hal Lingerman	*The Healing Energies of Music*	Quest Books 1983
Paul Newham	*The Singing Cure*	Rider Books 1993
Jonathan Goldman	*Healing Sounds*	Element 1992
Leah Maggie Garfield	*Sound Medicine*	Celestial Arts 1987
Stephen Halpern	*Sound Health*	Harper & Row 1985
John Beaulieu	*Music and Sound in the Healing Arts*	Station Hill Press 1987
Randall McClellan	*The Healing Forces of Music*	Element 1991
Michael Harner	*The Way of the Shaman*	Harper Collins 1990

Index

(numbers in italics refer to diagrams)